Sincerely
Helen Hayes

and
Merry Christmas
from Tom

A Gift of Joy

A GIFT

WITH LEWIS FUNKE

HELEN HAYES

OF JOY

Published by M. Evans and Company, Inc., *New York*
and distributed in association with
J. B. Lippincott Company, *Philadelphia and New York*

Library of Congress Catalog Card Number: 65-24466

Designed by Edward Gorey

Printed in the United States of America

ACKNOWLEDGMENTS

Thanks are due to the following authors, publishers, and agents for permission to use the material indicated:

George Allen & Unwin Ltd. for an excerpt from THE GARDENER'S YEAR by Karel Capek.

Anderson House for an excerpt from *Mary of Scotland* by Maxwell Anderson. Copyright 1933 by Maxwell Anderson. Copyright renewed 1960 by Gilda Anderson, Alan Anderson, Terence Anderson, Quentin Anderson, and Hesper A. Levenstein. All rights reserved. Reprinted by permission of Anderson House.

Bloch Publishing Company for an excerpt from A FAITH FOR MODERNS by Rabbi Robert Gordis.

Jonathan Cape Limited and the Executors of the Laurence Housman Estate for an excerpt from *Victoria Regina* by Laurence Housman.

Chatto & Windus Ltd. for excerpts from SWANN'S WAY by Marcel Proust, translated by C. K. Scott Moncrieff.

The Curtis Publishing Company for an excerpt from "The Child Who Never Grew" by Pearl S. Buck, originally published in the LADIES' HOME JOURNAL, Copyright 1950 by The Curtis Publishing Company.

Miss Helen Deutsch for "The White Magnolia Tree." Copyright 1957 by Helen Deutsch.

The Dial Press, Inc. for an excerpt reprinted from AMERICAN CHILD by Paul Engle. Copyright © 1945, 1956 by Paul Engle and used with the permission of the publishers, The Dial Press, Inc.

Doubleday & Company, Inc. for "The Glory of the Garden" from RUDYARD KIPLING'S VERSE: DEFINITIVE EDITION. Copyright 1911 by Rudyard Kipling. Reprinted by permission of Mrs. George Bambridge and Doubleday & Company, Inc.; and for excerpts from THE SUMMING UP by W. Somerset Maugham. Copyright 1938 by W. Somerset Maugham. Reprinted by permission of Doubleday & Company, Inc.

Dover Publications, Inc. for an excerpt from Karel Capek: THE GARDENER'S YEAR, Dover Publications, Inc., New York.

Mrs. Norma Millay Ellis for "Recuerdo" and "God's World" by Edna St. Vincent Millay. From COLLECTED POEMS. Harper & Row. Copyright 1913, 1922, 1940, 1950 by Edna St. Vincent Millay.

Faber & Faber Ltd. for "Autobiography" from COLLECTED POEMS by Louis MacNeice; for "What Are Years?" from COLLECTED POEMS BY MARIANNE MOORE; and for "I Think Continually of Those" from COLLECTED POEMS by Stephen Spender.

Harcourt, Brace & World, Inc. for "i thank You God for most this amazing" copyright, 1950, by E. E. Cummings. Reprinted from his volume POEMS 1923-1954 by permission of Harcourt, Brace & World, Inc.; and for an excerpt from "Street Haunting" in THE DEATH OF THE MOTH AND

OTHER ESSAYS by Virginia Woolf, copyright 1942, by Harcourt, Brace & World, Inc. and reprinted with their permission.

Harper & Row, Publishers, Incorporated for pp. 241-248 Act III of *The Skin of Our Teeth* in THREE PLAYS by Thornton Wilder. Copyrights 1942 by Thornton Wilder. Reprinted by special permission of the author and Harper & Row, Publishers.

Miss Helen Hayes for an excerpt from WAR BUGS by Charles MacArthur; and for an excerpt from *The Front Page* by Ben Hecht and Charles MacArthur, copyright 1928 by Ben Hecht and Charles MacArthur.

Mrs. Rose C. Hecht for an excerpt from *The Front Page*, copyright 1928 by Ben Hecht and Charles MacArthur.

William Heinemann Ltd. for an excerpt from MAINLY ON THE AIR by Sir Max Beerbohm.

The Jewish Theological Seminary of America for "The Night is Not Dark" by Rabbi Moshe Davis and Victor Ratner.

Alfred A. Knopf, Inc. for an excerpt from LETTERS OF H. L. MENCKEN. ⓒ Copyright 1962 by Alfred A. Knopf, Inc. Reprinted by permission; and for an excerpt from THE PROPHET. Copyright 1923 by Kahlil Gibran. Renewed 1951 by Administrators C. T. A. of Kahlil Gibran Estate and Mary G. Gibran. Reprinted from THE PROPHET by Kahlil Gibran by permission of Alfred A. Knopf, Inc.; and for an excerpt from MAINLY ON THE AIR by Max Beerbohm. Copyright 1946 by Max Beerbohm. Reprinted by permission of Alfred A. Knopf, Inc.; and for an excerpt from BUDDENBROOKS by Thomas Mann. Copyright 1952 by Alfred A. Knopf, Inc. Reprinted by permission.

The Macmillan Company for "My Windows" reprinted with permission of The Macmillan Company from PENELOPE AND OTHER POEMS by Sister M. Madeleva. Copyright 1927 by Sister M. Madeleva. Renewed 1955 by Sister M. Madeleva; and for "What Are Years?" Reprinted with permission of The Macmillan Company from WHAT ARE YEARS by Marianne Moore. Copyright 1941 by Marianne Moore; and for "The Voice of God" reprinted with permission of The Macmillan Company from COLLECTED POEMS by James Stephens. Copyright 1915 by The Macmillan Company. Renewed 1943 by James Stephens; and for "The Whisperer" reprinted with permission of The Macmillan Company from COLLECTED POEMS by James Stephens. Copyright 1909 by The Macmillan Company; and for "Lights" reprinted with permission of The Macmillan Company from COLLECTED POEMS by Sara Teasdale. Copyright 1917 by The Macmillan Company. Renewed 1945 by Mamie T. Wheless; and for "Return to a Country House" and "Grace Before Sleep" reprinted with permission of The Macmillan Company from COLLECTED POEMS by Sara Teasdale. Copyright 1933 by The Macmillan Company. Renewed 1961 by Guaranty Trust Co. of New York; and for "When You are Old" and "The Lake Isle of Innisfree" reprinted with permission of The Macmillan Company from COLLECTED POEMS by William Butler Yeats. Copyright 1906 by The Macmillan Company. Renewed 1934 by William Butler Yeats.

Macmillan & Co. Ltd. for "The Voice of God" and "The Whisperer" from COLLECTED POEMS by James Stephens. Reprinted by permission of Mrs. Iris Wise and Macmillan & Co. Ltd.

The New York Times for an excerpt from "The Meaning of Place" by Sean O'Faolain. ⓒ 1964 by The New York Times Company. Reprinted by permission.

W. W. Norton & Company, Inc. for an excerpt from *The Trojan Women*, reprinted from THREE GREEK PLAYS. Translated and with introductions by Edith Hamilton. By permission of W. W. Norton & Company, Inc. Copyright 1937 by W. W. Norton & Company, Inc. Copyright renewed 1965 by Doris Fielding Reid; and for an excerpt from "Mind and Spirit" reprinted from THE GREEK WAY by Edith Hamilton. By permission of W. W. Norton & Company, Inc. Copyright 1930, 1943 by W. W. Norton & Company, Inc. Copyright renewed 1958 by Edith Hamilton.

Harold Ober Associates, Inc. for an excerpt from THE CHILD WHO NEVER GREW by Pearl S. Buck. Published by The John Day Company, Inc.

Sean O'Faolain for an excerpt from "The Meaning of Place."

Oxford Universiy Press, Inc. for "Autobiography" from EIGHTY-FIVE POEMS by Louis MacNeice. © 1959 by Louis MacNeice. Reprinted by permission of Oxford University Press, Inc.

Mrs. Ella Tarbell Price for "Work" by Ida Tarbell.

Random House, Inc. for an excerpt from *Biography*, by S. N. Behrman. Copyright 1932, 1933 and renewed 1960 by S. N. Behrman. Reprinted by permission of Random House, Inc.; for excerpts from SWANN'S WAY by Marcel Proust. Copyright 1928 and renewed 1956 by The Modern Library, Inc. Reprinted from REMEMBRANCE OF THINGS PAST, by Marcel Proust, by permission of Random House, Inc.; for "I Think Continually of Those." Copyright 1934 and renewed 1961 by Stephen Spender. Reprinted from COLLECTED POEMS 1928-1953, by Stephen Spender, by permission of Random House, Inc.; and for excerpts from *The Glass Menagerie*, by Tennessee Williams. Copyright 1945 by Tennessee Williams and Edwina D. Williams. Reprinted by permission of Random House, Inc.

St. Anthony's Guild for "In Desert Places" from A QUESTION OF LOVERS AND OTHER POEMS printed by St. Anthony Guild Press, Paterson, N. J. Copyright 1935 by Sister M. Madeleva of the Congregation of the Holy Cross.

Charles Scribner's Sons for excerpts from *Dear Brutus* (copyright 1922 J. M. Barrie, renewal copyright 1950 Lady Cynthia Asquith); for an excerpt from *What Every Woman Knows* (copyright 1918 Charles Scribner's Sons; renewal copyright 1946 Cynthia Asquith); for excerpts from *Harriet* by Florence E. Ryerson and Colin Clements (copyright 1942, 1943 by Florence Ryerson Clements and Colin Clements); and for "O World" from POEMS by George Santayana. Used by permission of Charles Scribner's Sons.

Martin Secker & Warburg Limited for an excerpt from BUDDENBROOKS by Thomas Mann.

Simon and Schuster, Inc. for an excerpt from A CHILD OF THE CENTURY by Ben Hecht. Copyright 1954 by Ben Hecht. Reprinted by permission of Simon & Schuster, Inc.

The Society of Authors and The Public Trustee for an excerpt from *Androcles and the Lion* by George Bernard Shaw.

The Viking Press, Inc. for "Paterfamilias" from TIMES THREE by Phyllis McGinley. Copyright 1954 by Phyllis McGinley. Reprinted by permission of The Viking Press, Inc.

A. P. Watt & Son for "The Glory of the Garden" from THE DEFINITIVE EDITION OF RUDYARD KIPLING'S VERSE, by permission of Mrs. George Bambridge and The Macmillan Company of Canada Ltd.; and for excerpts from THE SUMMING UP by W. Somerset Maugham, by permission of Mr. Maugham and William Heinemann Ltd.; and for "When You Are Old" and "The Lake Isle of Innisfree" from COLLECTED POEMS OF W. B. YEATS, by permission of Mr. M. B. Yeats and The Macmillan Company of Canada Ltd.

The World Publishing Company for "She Did Not Know How To Be Famous" from PARTY OF ONE by Clifton Fadiman. Copyright © 1955 by Clifton Fadiman. Published by arrangement with The World Publishing Company, Cleveland and New York; and for an excerpt from "In Praise of Quotation" from ANY NUMBER CAN PLAY by Clifton Fadiman. Copyright © 1957 by Clifton Fadiman. Published by arrangement with The World Publishing Company, Cleveland and New York.

Yale University Press for an excerpt from A TOUCH OF THE POET. Reprinted by permission of Carlotta Monterey O'Neill and Yale University Press from A TOUCH OF THE POET by Eugene O'Neill. Copyright 1957 by Carlotta Monterey O'Neill.

For James MacArthur

CONTENTS

Introduction

In the beginning was the Word,
And the Word was with God,
And the Word was God.

I HAVE been misinterpreting those lines from St. John
with great satisfaction ever since I first heard them
in my childhood. At the start I really did misunder-
stand them—but when their true mystical significance was
explained to me later on I simply rejected it. It pleased
me to believe that St. John thought enough of words to deify
them. For I am a lover of words. Other people's to be sure
—personally, I never know what to do with the things.

One has to grow up with good talk in order to form the
habit of it. In the Hayes family, talk, though incessant, was
limited—and physical. Nobody ever bothered to reach for
the exact word. Everyone fell back on gesture, mugging,
miming. I can remember the many times in the middle of a

dinner when my mother, my Aunt Mamie, and Graddy Hayes would leap to their feet and cavort around the table in active description of an acquaintance encountered that day on F Street in my native Washington, D.C. My father would eat on, never looking up. But I was always carried away by the show.

Actually, I suppose, I did inherit a love of words from my grandfather, Patrick Hayes, who, I was repeatedly reminded by my mother and Aunt Mamie, was such an avid reader that if he saw a piece of torn newspaper—any piece of paper with printing on it—he had to read it. They also said that he was a great authority on Shakespeare and that in the last years of his life he was attempting to translate him into Gaelic. I've sometimes wondered whether that story had not been one of the Hayes sisters' attempts to be swell. Certainly, there was only one bit of poetry handed down to me from my scholarly Grandpa, and that was a spirited marching song delivered with a horrendous brogue:

> Be good, be good, me fayther said,
> Tho' the way be long and shtarmy;
> Some day you may be prisidint
> Or gineral in the army.

Perhaps I inherited from him my addiction for anything with words on it. I once went to an optometrist and got so taken with reading the eye chart and an unfinished quotation on it that I forgot all about the glasses I came for and set the poor clerk on a chase for the complete quotation.

I was introduced to words in the theater, naturally, since words are its main concern, or should be. It was lucky for me that I fell in with good company there at an early age, good playwrights whose lines I learned as a job, friends who pressed good books on me, friends who undertook my education. These people filled my head with literature that was often beyond my capacity—but whether or not I understood what I was reading, I was acquiring a taste for good words.

How wise that fine acting coach, Constance Collier, was when a parent complained because her eleven-year-old daughter had been given Keats' "Ode to a Nightingale" to memorize. It is intricate, sensuous, and surely incomprehensible to a youngster. Understandably startled and a little alarmed, the parent said, "Don't you think that's too much for the child? She'll never understand what the words mean." To which Constance replied, "Oh, that doesn't matter, dear. Just think that when she's playing alone, or when she's walking home from school alone, or when she just has nothing else to do, instead of some cheap little tune running through her head, she'll have those lovely words in there."

Words are the keys to thoughts and ideas. And, so, while I was developing a taste for words, I was also developing a taste for thoughts and ideas expressed by minds far better than mine. And I was storing up strength to meet the bright and the dark of the future. Years ago, on *The Chief*, I crossed the continent from Hollywood with a beautiful woman I knew slightly. She was in the last stage of tuberculosis and was going back to her home in England to die. She had been a successful ballroom dancer with the usual string of admirers and had amassed a pretty collection of jewelry. When we were under way, she sent a message begging me to come to her compartment. Conversation was impossible since even the effort to whisper left her spent—but it was not conversation she wished. Very soon she indicated by a nod to her maid that she was ready for what I imagined was a daily ritual. The maid placed a large leather jewel case beside her mistress, unlocked and opened it. For the next hour and a half I was required to take each piece from the drawers, hold it up to the light, and turn it this way and that while she feverishly studied first the jewel and then my face for a reaction. My exhibition of unalloyed delight was one of my finer performances. But I really wanted to cry. All that life had given this woman to hold on to was this box of hard, bright objects we were playing with. This was all that was left to her to help her through her final crisis. And in the dark, when one needs comfort most, she couldn't even see her treasures.

I was young then and wearing my entire jewel collection —a one-and-a-quarter carat engagement ring and a diamond-chip wedding band—but I felt so rich all of a sudden that I was ashamed of myself. Already I had amassed quite a fortune inside my head—phrases my husband, Charlie, had uttered when he was making love that *way* outsparkled any diamonds he might have put on my fingers, or those shown me by this poor woman. And the gifts from Shakespeare, Shaw, Max Anderson, and James M. Barrie—these were only a few. I'd had to learn their words as a job—but I had hung on to them.

It is reassuring to have a hoard—even a small one—of good thoughts well expressed, stashed away in one's head for those crises that must come to every life. After our daughter died my husband struggled for a long time to recapture some lines of poetry that glowed just out of reach in his memory. He wanted to put them on her grave. It helped us both immeasurably when he found the lines in "Epitaph on Elizabeth, L. H." by Ben Jonson, and could make his last pretty gift to Mary:

Underneath this stone doth lie
As much beauty as could die

We rely upon the poets, the philosophers, and the play-wrights to articulate what most of us can only feel, in joy or sorrow. They illuminate the thoughts for which we only grope; they give us the strength and balm we cannot find within ourselves. Whenever I feel my courage wavering I rush to them. They give me the wisdom of acceptance, the will and resilience to push on. They enable me to see that I am not alone, that others have known similar problems. I'm so grateful for this inheritance, this legacy—this gift of joy—that makes me feel as rich as Croesus and enables me to say with Emerson:

I am the owner of the sphere,
Of the seven stars and the solar year,
Of Caesar's hand, and Plato's brain,
Of Lord Christ's heart, and Shakespeare's strain.

Delmore Schwartz has said: "Only the past is immortal." To which Clifton Fadiman in his essay "In Praise of Quotation" has added: "But its immortality is not uncondi-tional. It cannot be kept alive solely by scholars and professional intellectuals. It must be kept alive by you and me. All mankind is but a carrier, and part of our precious burden consists of things that have been said perfectly. To repeat them, appositely and not too frequently, is to add to the general stock of knowledge and pleasure. Indeed it is a kind of good citizenship, for we are all citizens of History, a country whose continually threatened borders we must be at any time prepared to defend. To still in ourselves the golden voices of the past is to regress toward the voiceless condition of the fishes."

I am a carrier of that precious burden. What follows, therefore, is a blend of reminiscence and quotation. I begin with the reminiscences that are dearest to me.

Charlie

'Twas on a Monday morning,
  Right early in the year,
That Charlie came to our town,
  The young Chevalier.

    An' Charlie, he's my darling,
    My darling, my darling,
    Charlie, he's my darling,
      The young Chevalier.

As he was walking up the street,
  The city for to view,
O there he spied a bonie lass
  The window looking through.
      An' Charlie, etc.

Sae light's he jumped up the stair,
  And tirl'd at the pin;
And wha sae ready as hersel'
  To let the laddie in.
      An' Charlie, etc.

17

He sets his Jenny on his knee,
All in his Highland dress;
For brawlie weel he ken'd the way
To please a bonie lass.
                    An' Charlie, etc.

CHARLIE MACARTHUR strolled into our town at the peak of the roaring Twenties. Almost immediately he was adopted by the New York wits and hunted by the town's Dianas. This young chevalier from Chicago had come well armed for conquest. He had wit, a dark, sloe-eyed kind of beauty, a stirring familiarity with violence, and he wove Homeric tales of the two great wars of the time, World War I and the one in Chicago gangland. He was elusive and, above all, he bore himself with a bland indifference. This was the Charlie the clever ones saw. The crowning glory of my life was that somehow I saw below the surface to the real Charlie and recognized him for my own true love.

The first time I met Charlie was at a late afternoon studio party given by the then-famous illustrator, Neysa McMein. I had been taken there by Marc Connelly, whom I happened to meet earlier on Fifth Avenue. Marc was the co-author of *To the Ladies*, in which I was appearing. Although I was already a star in the theater, I was leading a most secluded life for an actress. I hardly knew a soul at the party. I sat in a corner going through the usual pantomime of listening and cocking my head at what was being said. And then a beautiful young man came up to me with a bag of peanuts in his hand and said, "Want a peanut?"

I was startled. But I answered correctly, "Yes, thank you." The young man poured several peanuts out of the bag into my hand. Then he smiled at me and said, "I wish they were emeralds." He asked to take me home. I forgot all about

Mr. Connelly, and everything else. Years later, to my regret and Charlie's, I told this story to an interviewer in Hollywood in an effort to be cooperative when I was being launched in films. It was repeated over and over again until it nearly drove Charlie out of his head. And so, years later, when he came home from the eastern theater of World War II, he did bring me a bag of emeralds from India. And he said, "I wish they were peanuts."

When I met Charlie, I was living in a three-room apartment with my mother and a friend, Jean Dixon. It was hardly a set-up for entertaining a beau. Charlie and I spent much of our courtship looking for places where we could be alone. He was quite imaginative about using the city around him. We spent a great deal of time riding ferries to Staten Island and taking trains up to Nyack, where we began our long walks along the river. Charlie loved Nyack. He had grown up there when his father was a minister at the old Missionary College on the hill overlooking the town. It was on one of our ferry trips that Charlie introduced me to Edna St. Vincent Millay's "Recuerdo."

We were very tired, we were very merry—
We had gone back and forth all night on the ferry.
It was bare and bright, and smelled like a stable—
But we looked into a fire, we leaned across a table,
We lay on a hill-top underneath the moon;
And the whistles kept blowing, and the dawn came soon.

We were very tired, we were very merry—
We had gone back and forth all night on the ferry;
And you ate an apple, and I ate a pear,
From a dozen of each we had bought somewhere;

And the sky went wan, and the wind came cold,
And the sun rose dripping, a bucketful of gold.

We were very tired, we were very merry,
We had gone back and forth all night on the ferry.
We hailed, "Good morrow, mother!" to a shawl-covered
    head,
And bought a morning paper, which neither of us read;
And she wept, "God bless you!" for the apples and pears,
And we gave her all our money but our subway fares.

Charlie and I had a rather long courtship. Also it was a
troubled one. Someone said that the community always tries
its best to pull lovers apart before, and keep them together
after, marriage. In our case the sides were sharply drawn
between my protectors, who feared that I would be run
over and squashed, and Charlie's admirers, who knew he
would be bored to death. It took all of Charlie's wisdom
to pilot us through their nonsensical interference.

We weren't married until after the opening of *The Front
Page* which Charlie wrote with Ben Hecht. It was in 1928.
I had already scored a great success in *Coquette* and Charlie had made up his mind that he wasn't going to marry
me until he had a triumph equal to mine. So, the opening
of *The Front Page* was the most important of my life. Jed
Harris, the producer of both *Coquette* and *The Front Page*,
closed my show for the night to enable me to attend the
premiere. I went to the theater in a state of terrible tension
and sat alone up in the balcony near a fire exit. I wanted
to be able to leave quickly after each act to report to Charlie
and Ben. They had elected to sit it out on the fire escape.

I wanted Charlie to have a success not only because I loved him but also because my future happiness depended on that night. The curtain went up and it wasn't long before the audience began warming to this rowdy play about the gentlemen of the press. They laughed and reacted enthusiastically. But my fears didn't diminish a bit until the great moment when Dorothy Stickney, in the role of Mollie Malloy, the prostitute, roared onto the stage like a high wind and tore into the scene with all her great talent. At the end of the scene she made her exit to one of the wildest ovations I've ever heard. People don't carry on like that today—the ovation went on for minutes and minutes and minutes and in that time, while the great music of applause and cheers was circling around my head, I knew that my future was assured. I raced out at the end of the act. The heroes of the night were huddled on the iron steps, all pinched and white in the half light. Reaching Charlie's arms in two bounds over the rickety fire escape grating I babbled wildly about the audience's reaction; how I had watched over the balcony railing—Charlie Chaplin in stitches, Heywood Broun slapping his knees and roaring, Woollcott puffing up like a blow-fish. "I bet he thinks he invented you," I said "and you should have seen . . ." Charlie silenced me the only way he could at that moment by holding me tight against his chest. Then he held me off and said, "Helen, will you marry me?" and I said, "You took the words right out of my mouth."

During all the years of our marriage, Charlie was a gallant lover. His letters were ardent, his gifts thoughtful. Charlie knew how to lift a woman's heart. I think this letter, written in the Carlton Hotel in Washington, D.C., in December 1943, speaks for itself.

Angel,

It's 5:30 A.M. and I've given up the idea of sleep so I might as well be writing you a letter. I've been alternately reading bad plays and thinking pleasantly of you and wishing you were here in my arms. I've been remembering so many things from our buggy ride to Fraunces Tavern on down the years—all my boobish love antics return to entertain me. I run upstairs in East 40th Street with you in my arms (I believe I could do it still without getting too much out of breath) and I see you coming down Madison Avenue in a little gray suit with a green orchid I sent you on your shoulder or wearing that awful Empire dress I brought you from Paris or that pretty postillion coat or standing on the dock when the Belgenland hove to when you told the newspaper boys we were engaged and I got slapped with Miss Frink's summons at the baggage pile. And the first time I ever kissed you in a cab and how you lied ever after when you said you didn't lean toward me first. And sitting up with you in Childs and going over the brow of yon hills in France and the fight about Molnar's picture and the swing at Syosset and the open fire at Otto Kahn's. And the Victrola I bought you for your birthday and the way your stomach felt at the Santa Barbara Biltmore when the embryo Mary was only a few weeks old, and how I rubbed your stomach later with cocoa butter and got my face slapped for further familiarities and how I nearly abandoned you on the street (or said I would abandon you) when you told me the waterbag might burst on the way to the hospital. And how I used to chase you around with a Leica whenever I caught you with your clothes off, and the time you posed with hat and fan. 536 Madison, with you frightening me stiff by telling me you were going to stay the night. The bed at 15 Park we were never going to sell. The time you got tight and gambled and were so gay at Barney Glazer's, and picking out the hat for Madelon Claudet and my horror the first time I went back and saw an old belle of mine in a bustle after a performance of Victoria. And my boobish names for. . . . And now I'll go to work. Don't worry about me. I hope I always have this particular form of insomnia. Thank you for a very pleasant night, my dearest, only love.

All this is so little of my happiness,

Charlie

Shortly after D-Day, I was looking out of the window of our house in Nyack when suddenly I saw him coming up the walk. My excitement was indescribable. And it was increased by something at once ludicrous and marvelously romantic. There Charlie was, in full uniform, his battle ribbons across his chest, his lieutenant-colonel's oak leaves on his shoulders—carrying a partly beat-up rose in his hand. He had plucked that rose in a garden in Normandy, and kept it in a container of water all the way home on the plane.

Charlie also understood human beings. And he was tolerant of their frailties. Once when I was railing against someone who hadn't behaved as I thought I might have in similar circumstances, he said to me, "Helen, I can never understand why we expect all human beings to behave the same. We don't expect a Great Dane to behave like a Pekinese, or a French poodle like a collie. They're all dogs but they are different kinds."

Old friends who might not see Charlie for long periods of time would return when they were in trouble. F. Scott Fitzgerald was one who'd appear when things had come close to unendurable. And Bob Benchley was another who came back to Charlie in his moments of despair. These friends knew that Charlie was never going to be righteous with them, that they would never be made aware of his sympathy. He just was going to be there, like a tape recorder, and they could talk and unburden themselves without getting anything back that might hurt or embarrass them.

I do not mean to imply that Charlie was a saint. He wasn't. He was full of mischief and laughter, and those who remember him can still spend nights on end regaling listeners with stories of their adventures with him. It also is true that from time to time he had a few more drinks than were good for him. I witnessed one bout that continues to astound me whenever I recall it. John Barrymore had been visiting Ben Hecht, who also lived in Nyack. After he'd started back to New York, he discovered that he didn't have any cigarettes. He stopped at our place. He wanted to borrow a pack. He left three days later.

Charlie adored Jack, who had a mind which, when it was in full flower, was something delightful to be exposed to. And, of course, John loved his alcohol. Before dinner that first night the two of them downed goodness-knows-how-much of the Scotch that was in the house. They polished off a great deal of wine at dinner, and after dinner they were at it again. When they ran out of scotch, they started on the bourbon, then rye; and when they ran out of those Charlie found a bottle of Calvados, which was all that was left in the house. Calvados is pure dynamite. I just sat there. I wasn't going to get up and say, "No more." I just watched in awe. I never saw two men put so much away. Charlie, who wasn't in the same league as John, was just managing to keep up. They got halfway through the bottle of Calvados when a discussion of Walt Whitman's "The Open Road" came up. This was one of Charlie's great favorites, and I was dispatched to his study to get a copy of Whitman's *Leaves of Grass*, which contains that poem, because Charlie wanted John to read it to him. John put on a pair of nickel-rimmed glasses—I hadn't seen anyone for years wearing those things. He turned the pages until he came to "The Open Road." Awash in alcohol, he complained, "I haven't read this bloody thing in years and it's bloody hard to read." With that he started. He read with such beauty, with never a hesitation over a word or an emphasis. It was like a concert. Charlie just reveled in it, loving it, and giving himself over to the lines—and I did too. These are the lines I remember most vividly.

From this hour I ordain myself loos'd of limits and
    imaginary lines,
Going where I list, my own master total and absolute,
Listening to others, considering well what they say,
Pausing, searching, receiving, contemplating,
Gently, but with undeniable will, divesting myself of
    the holds that would hold me.

I inhale great draughts of space,
The east and the west are mine, and the north and south
    are mine.

I am larger, better than I thought,
I did not know I held so much goodness.

All seems beautiful to me,
I can repeat over to men and women You have done
    such good to me I would do the same to you,
I will recruit for myself and you as I go,
I will scatter myself among men and women as I go,
I will toss a new gladness and roughness among them,

Whoever denies me it shall not trouble me,
Whoever accepts me he or she shall be blessed and shall
    bless me.

There is a postscript to that night. Sometime the next
afternoon Charlie and Jack wobbled down to where I was
sitting beside our swimming pool. They wanted nothing
so much as a cold, cold dip, but the water seemed tepid
to them. So Charlie called the local ice company and ordered
its entire supply, two truckloads of ice. The trucks were
backed up to the pool and out shot the great blocks. Jack,
lolling on his ice floe, was most appreciative and said he
felt like a fly in a highball.

Charlie always had a clear picture of himself and his place
in the world. "He was born," Ben Hecht said, "without the
illusion of permanence. He knew at the beginning the road's
end." Although Charlie never brooded about death, he was
always aware of it, and felt a close kinship for those who
knew how to meet it with gallantry. He loved, for instance,
the death scene in *Cyrano de Bergerac*. He told me that he
never read it without tears coming to his eyes.

When Charlie's own time came, he met it with a quip.
Lying in the hospital as the end neared, he awoke from a
deep sleep, sized up the gathering of doctors and nurses
around his bedside and asked, "What the hell is this—a block
party?" A few moments later he announced, "If you sawbones
will cease your attentions and vamoose, I promise to put a
feather in the cap of medicine. I'll walk out of here on my
own two legs."

As for Charlie's success in the theater, he was constantly
conscious of how fleeting it could be, how fickle public
approval could be, how transitory. He knew this from the
outset. Even when I first met him—when he was just on

the way up and people like H. L. Mencken, George Jean Nathan, and others had great hopes for his potential—he was preparing himself for the way down. In the small apartment he shared with Bob Benchley he had hanging on the wall of his room a cartoon of a tree on a high peak. It was leafless, twisted and tortured, having been buffeted by the wind and the elements. Streaking down toward it was a bolt of lightning. Underneath, the caption read, "Fame."

One of his favorite verses from Shakespeare dealt with the same subject.

Time hath, my lord, a wallet at his back,
Wherein he puts alms for oblivion,
A great-siz'd monster of ingratitudes.
Those scraps are good deeds past, which are devour'd
As fast as they are made, forgot as soon
As done. Perseverance, dear my lord,
Keeps honour bright. To have done is to hang
Quite out of fashion, like a rusty mail
In monumental mock'ry. Take the instant way;
For honour travels in a strait so narrow
Where one but goes abreast. Keep then the path,
For emulation hath a thousand sons
That one by one pursue. If you give way,
Or hedge aside from the direct forthright,
Like to an ent'red tide they all rush by
And leave you hindmost;
Or, like a gallant horse fall'n in first rank,
Lie there for pavement to the abject rear,
O'errun and trampled on. Then what they do in present,
Though less than yours in past, must o'ertop yours;
For Time is like a fashionable host,
That slightly shakes his parting guest by th' hand,
And with his arms outstretch'd as he would fly

Grasps in the comer. The welcome ever smiles,
And farewell goes out sighing. Let not virtue seek
Remuneration for the thing it was!
For beauty, wit,
High birth, vigour of bone, desert in service,
Love, friendship, charity, are subjects all
To envious and calumniating Time.
One touch of nature makes the whole world kin,
That all with one consent praise new-born gauds,
Though they are made and moulded of things past,
And give to dust that is a little gilt
More laud than gilt o'erdusted.

Balzac once said that no one should ever congratulate an author on getting out a new book. Instead, he said, they should commiserate with him for having spent a little more of his talent and his productive force. When Charlie's productive force slackened I was miserable for him. I knew there was much that he still wanted to say and yet, somehow, he was unable to say it in a manner that pleased him. I was sad for him because I knew how troubled he was. One night when Charlie was especially blue, he disappeared into his room and I was alone with F. Scott Fitzgerald, who had come on a visit. I said something about my sadness to Scott, a man who knew his own despairs, his own loss of the productive force. I said I knew how unhappy Charlie must be because he wasn't writing and Scott said something I never forgot and which consoled me. He said, "Helen, what difference does it make whether he produces masterpieces for four people around a dinner table or for four million readers of *The Saturday Evening Post*? The chances are that those people at the dinner table understand and appreciate him more than the four million. They have benefited and they have been enormously enriched." Scott added something else that I have always cherished. "There are some people," he said, "who have to *do* in order to make their mark. They have to perform, they have to contribute. And there are some people who only have to *be*. Charlie is one who just has to *be*."

Years later I was to know that, though Charlie did not leave a great body of work, he, nevertheless, left words to make men cheer. Thirty years had passed before *The Front Page* was translated into French and produced in Paris. It was a great success and I was urged to go and see it. Somehow, I kept putting the idea aside. The play ran and ran and finally, just before I went into rehearsal with *Shakespeare Revisited*, I got on a plane. I just had to see and hear for myself. I had cabled my son Jim, who was in London with his wife, to come over and meet me. Paris was in the throes of the Algerian crisis when we arrived and everyone seemed terribly disgruntled. The City of Light had become the city of kicks in the shin. I never saw people so angry at one another. When I got off the plane, I found that there was a taxi strike and getting out of the airport was almost impossible. People walked in the streets with a kind of fury in their eyes and on Boulevard Haussmann there were students sitting interfering with the traffic. But in the theater the power of the words was supreme. At the end of the first act these same Frenchmen were slapping each other on the back, roaring with innocent glee. Because there *is* a great innocence in *The Front Page*. It seemed that everyone felt it and was refreshed in spirit. I watched Jim and his wife enjoying themselves too—and I knew that Charlie would have been pleased.

The scene that follows takes place in the press room of the criminal court building in Chicago. Reporters are sitting around playing poker. They are awaiting the early morning execution of a man named Earl Williams who has been found guilty of murder. At this point Mollie Malloy enters.

MURPHY. Hello, Mollie!

ENDICOTT. Well, well! Here's the Moll.

WILSON. Hello, kid! How's the old liver?

MC CUE. *(With bogus accent)* Shure, and how are yez, Mollie?

MOLLIE. *(Crossing down Center)* I've been looking for you bums.

MURPHY. Going to pay a call on Williams?

SCHWARTZ. He's just across the courtyard.

KRUGER. Better hurry up—he hasn't got all night.

MC CUE. Yes, he has!

ENDICOTT. Say, Mollie, those were pretty roses you sent Earl. What do you want done with them tomorrow morning?

MOLLIE. *(Low and tense)* A lot of wise guys, ain't you? Well, you know what I think of you—all of you.

MURPHY. Now,—keep your pants on, Mollie.

MOLLIE. *(To MURPHY)* If you was worth breaking my fingernails on, I'd tear your puss wide open.

MURPHY. What you sore about, sweetheart? Wasn't that a swell story we give you?

MOLLIE. You cheap crumbs have been making a fool out of me long enough!

ENDICOTT. Now what kind of language is that?

BENSINGER. She oughtn't to be allowed in here!

MOLLIE. I never said I loved Earl Williams and was willing to marry him on the gallows! You made that up! And all that other bunk about my being his soulmate and having a love nest with him! *(She crosses up Center.)*

MC CUE. Well, didn't you?

ENDICOTT. You've been sucking around that cuckoo

ever since he's been in the death house. Everybody knows you're his affinity!

MOLLIE. (*Turns to* ENDICOTT) That's a lie! I met Mr. Williams just once in my life, when he was wandering around in the rain without his hat and coat on, like a sick dog. The day before the shooting. And I went up to him like any human being would, and I asked him what was the matter, and he told me about being fired after working at the same place twenty-two years and I brought him up to my rooms because it was warm there. (*She crosses Left Center.*)

ENDICOTT. Did he have the two dollars?

MURPHY. Aw, put it on a victrola record.

MOLLIE. Just because you want to fill your lying papers with a lot of dirty scandal, you got to crucify him and make a bum out of me!

ENDICOTT. Aw, go on!

MOLLIE. I tell you he just sat there talking to me—all night! He just sat there talking to me, and never once laid a hand on me, and in the morning he went away, and I never seen him again till the day of the trial.

ENDICOTT. Tell us what you told the jury!

(*The* REPORTERS *laugh.*)

MOLLIE. Go on, laugh! Damn you! Sure I was his witness—the only one he had. Yes, me! Mollie Malloy! A Clark Street tart! I was the only one with guts enough to stand up for him! And that's why you're persecuting me!! Because he treated me decent, and not like an animal, and I said so!

ENDICOTT. Why didn't you adopt him instead of letting him run around shooting policemen?

SCHWARTZ. Suppose that cop had been your own brother?

MOLLIE. I wish to God it had been one of you!

MURPHY. Say, what's the idea of this song and dance, anyhow! This is the press room. We're busy.

SCHWARTZ. Go on home.

MURPHY. Or go and see your boy friend.

MC CUE. Yah—he's got a nice room.

ENDICOTT. He won't have it long. He's left a call for seven A.M.

MOLLIE. *(Crosses up Right Center before speaking)* It's a wonder a bolt of lightning don't come through the ceiling and strike you all *dead!! (She crosses Right to window. At the sound of the GALLOWS)* What's that? Oh, my God! *(Begins to cry, covering her face with her hands.)*

BENSINGER. *(Rising)* Say, what's the idea? *(To the* OTHERS*)* She oughtn't to be allowed in here.

MOLLIE. *(Taking cue "idea")* Talking that way about a fellow that's going to die.

ENDICOTT. Now don't get hysterical.

MOLLIE. *(Sobbing)* Shame on you! Shame on you!

SCHWARTZ. Come on, Mollie, go on home. Be a good girl.

MOLLIE. A poor little crazy fellow. Sitting there alone, with the Angel of Death beside him. *(She turns and takes a step Left)* And you cracking jokes.

MURPHY. *(Getting up meaningly)* Listen, if you don't shut up, I'll give you something good to cry about! *(He crosses and grabs* MOLLIE's *arm.)*

MOLLIE. Keep your dirty hands off me!

MURPHY. *(He turns her around and pushes her to the door up Right)* Outside, *bum!*

MOLLIE. *(Going through the door)* You low down heels! You dirty punks! *(Exits.)*

Ben Hecht said Charlie was in love with death. But this was a wrong guess. On the contrary—it seems to me that

Charlie was so in love with life that he lived it too greedily and too hard. He was blithely indifferent to death and neither courted it nor tried to stave it off—he accepted it as one does a familiar part of one's everyday life, like sleeping. At the age of twenty-one, he began to live intimately with death. He fought his way through every major engagement in which the American doughboys participated in World War I. Here is the beginning of his chapter on Chateau-Thierry from *War Bugs*.

The Germans were still running when we got to Chateau-Thierry. From the looks of things it might have been Hallowe'en. Both sides had made a bum out of the town. Nothing was left but latitude, longitude, and broken brick.

We trotted through the rubbish in the general direction of the front. Up hill and down, cannoneers to the wheels, and how do you like the war by now? By sunset we reached a marked-down forest near Montreuil-aux-Lions, until a few hours before the shelter of the Twenty-sixth Division, now burning in the wake of the war. It was a litter of dead horses and men, broken wagons, dirty blankets, shelter halves, mess kits, rifles, and miscellaneous junk to the value of three Liberty Loans. The day was hot, the air clammy with death.

Yet it's an ill wind that gathers no moss. For once we were able to salvage all the food and equipment we wanted, including some curious luxuries. Somebody found a phonograph and one record. For the following twelve hours the deep tangled wildwood rang with the "Gamblin' Man Blues," over and over and *over* again.

The officers had a foolish notion that the woods ought to be tidied up before we went out to play. A few burials were ordered. Hunting for picks and shovels the boys discovered a beer saloon, and there was an immediate

and highly insubordinate stampede. The officers ran
after and ordered Madame not to sell a drop. Madame
took them seriously, waved her arms at the thirsty, and
screamed "Feeneesh, feeneesh, feeneesh!" like the silly
goose that she was.

It looked like a dry night until Porch Climber discovered a shell hole six feet in diameter in the rear wall
of the saloon. Because the café was built on a slope the
hole, although on the first floor, was thirty feet above
the ground. Porch ascended like a Human Fly, using
finger nails, teeth, and toes.

Rush Dyer was sent to the front door of the café to
divert Madame. This was difficult, as Madame was in a
temper, and he had to resort to amorous ways and
means. "*Non, non,* NON!" said Madame. "OUI!" said Rush
firmly. Amid the exchange of vows Porch Climber ascended and stealthily lowered a case of Hennessey
Three Star. That was more than enough, but Porch
Climber was too thorough to quit while there was anything left. A case of Calvados descended, some beverage
called Marc, several cases of wine, Triple-Sec, Bene-
dictine, Scotch, and cordials, until all of Madame's store-
room stock was in her back yard. Incidentally her "*nons*"
were getting fainter, so it was Heaven's judgment, probably.

We found wheelbarrows and pushed the booty back
to camp. Several officers were about, but we disguised
the loads with gunnysacks and swore loudly at the in-
justice of doing day labour after such a long and bitter
hike. By dinner time we had cached nearly six hundred
bottles of various intoxicants halfway up the hill across
the road from the camp. Wild Bill Sloan was elected
bartender, and the word went out—very cautiously—that
the panic was on. Looting rhymed too well with shooting to advertise the party.

There would have been no trouble at all if Rush hadn't

sampled the Calvados with Madame and now pro-
nounced it ordinary American corn whiskey. This point
was debated by Bill, considered an expert because he
came from Tennessee. Rush's opinion was simply that of
an amateur, said Bill, and proceeded to prove it.

The argument became bitter. Rush offered to drink
an entire bottle, intending to identify the stuff by the
effect it produced. This reasonable plan was misunder-
stood by Wild Bill, who considered that a race was on—
and offered to spot him a bottle and drink the entire
case.

Now Calvados is peculiar stuff. Veteran French
boozers limit themselves to a tablespoonful, and at that,
end up licking policemen and setting fire to the Arc de
Triomphe. So in fifteen minutes curious things were
happening. Bill had killed a bottle and a half—Rush a
bottle, claiming that an old case of lockjaw had come
back on him. The rest of the boys were smoothing
individual bottles more temperately.

Rush, whom we knew to be a Southerner from Mis-
sissippi, began talking in hard Northern style and spoke
long and circumstantially of his life among the Eskimos.
For no reason he recited the list of his loves and made
all of them out to be daughters of Senators and Gov-
ernors.

Wild Bill cocked his automatic and offered to bore
places for earrings in anybody present; he was not
angry, he explained, merely expert. Herb Mooney was
discovered taking off his shoes. He said that it was very
late and that he didn't want to wake his wife. When
last seen he was tiptoeing down the hillside carrying
what looked like a couple of violin cases—if violin cases
had heels. Bill had his ear to the ground by that time
and thought he could discern the approach of reve-
nooers. We had to disarm him. In time we slept where
we fell.

Oh, oh, oh, and oh, what a morning! We picked ourselves out of trees, shell holes, mud puddles and from
under the gun carriages and tried to stand up while
Captain Stone laid into us. Fortunately Madame had not
yet discovered her principal loss. The captain passed to
the subject of identification tags, his favourite topic,
and spoke of their use in the awful event of death. All
of us felt that he was completely nuts. Death would have
been a luxury at the moment.

Here is part of Ben Hecht's eulogy for Charlie.

Helen tells me that Charlie liked, in his last year, to
have people read aloud to him a few paragraphs I wrote.
I read them to him again—with a few minor alterations.
I hope they won't disturb him. He was a fellow always
quickly disturbed by a wrong adjective.

. . . . the most fun of the show around me was those
with whom I shared it. Of these, my friend Charles
MacArthur was the most active. We wrote plays and
movies together. But our literary work was only a side-
line of our relationship. Even the adventures we shared
in Mexico and other spots of the earth were a lesser
factor.

Our friendship was founded on a mutual obsession.
We were both obsessed with our youthful years. I had
no more interest in Charlie's past than he in mine. But
for twenty-five years we assisted each other in behaving
as if these pasts had never vanished. We remained newspaper reporters and continued to keep our hats on before
the boss, drop ashes on the floor, and disdain all practical people.

But it is difficult for two grown men to continue playing games and palavering as if they were marking time
in some press room. Thus, since MacArthur was hotly
in love with the theatre we added play-writing to our
relationship, and later movie writing . . . .

We finished only a few of the plays we started. I sigh, remembering the first acts we threw away, the merry plots we lost or forgot. We were lavish fellows and we gave no damn for anything except our youth, and how to keep it going in the teeth and bald spots, and graying sideburns, and, God forgive us, even paunches.

It was Charlie who lured me to Nyack. He had been raised on a hill outside the town where his father tended a tabernacle. The elder MacArthur was a handsome man, with the Bibles [both of them] roaring in his head.

Looking around for someplace where we might write a play without a city interruption, Charlie remembered Nyack. In Nyack, he said, we would find peace and inspiration. We went there, and rented a Girls' College that had recently gone bankrupt. Here we lived in some fifty bedrooms for the summer. One day when we were eating a picnic lunch on a hilltop, our families decided to move permanently to Nyack.

MacArthur was a man of quicker perception than anyone I have ever known. He seemed without psychological attitudes and yet he was as aware of people as if he had eavesdropped on them in an analyst's office.

The same paradox marked his allure. He seemed never interested in attracting anyone, yet people scampered toward him as if pulled by a magnet.

Alec Woollcott who loved him, said to me once. "What a perfect world this would be if it were peopled by MacArthurs."

I know what he meant. It would be a world in which people charmed each other and let each other alone . . . . in which people knew each other's secrets but never intruded on each other—one of the many attractive things about my friend was his modesty. In the many years I knew him, I never heard him utter a boast on any subject.

Fame

MONTAIGNE has said that with great merit and even greater modesty one can remain unknown for a long time. Yet I wonder how often those who have overcome their modesty have had their merit recognized; have, in short, become famous. And if they have, how often must they wonder over the price. And how often do they yearn again for the joy in anonymity which Emily Dickinson expressed:

> I'm nobody! Who are you?
> Are you nobody, too?
> Then there's a pair of us—don't tell!
> They'd banish us, you know.
>
> How dreary to be somebody!
> How public, like a frog
> To tell your name the livelong day
> To an admiring bog!

It has become fashionable to psychologize and say that those who seek fame are, secretly, hostile types. Supposedly, these hostilities begin with the child's first awareness that his parents are stronger than he is, and his lack of reassurance that he will one day be their equal. Other theories cite failure-prone fathers, mistreatment, loneliness, poverty, and the loss of a parent as causes of the kind of hostility that motivates us towards fame. Well, I don't know. I'm not aware that I have a whole set of hostilities beyond the norm. And I don't remember as a child dreaming of becoming famous in the theater to get even with anyone. Sure, there probably were times when I had been hurt, when I'd had a scrap with a friend, when I felt that I was not beloved by my mother, or when I was being disciplined, that I may have had daydreams of going out and getting famous and bowing to the crowd and being ever so gracious about it all. There may have been moments when I used to fancy myself so big a figure that I could turn the other cheek—you know, show them what it was like to be really great yet good and loyal and kind. But I don't remember that the need to achieve fame was an overpowering private fantasy with which I lived. The fact is that, other than those trivial recollections I have just mentioned, the thought of fame itself for vengeful purposes never crossed my mind. I wanted to be famous only because in my profession fame is directly related to how good you are. Fame in the theater means material rewards at the box office, and it also means that you have a choice of the better roles. And this is very important to an actor who is creative and who is seeking growth.

But what fame demands of you, once you have achieved it, is both onerous and bothersome. Even though it is all part of my work, it has never ceased to bother me. I never knew how to do it well—to be famous. I was not trained to it because I grew up in the theater when actors and great stars simply didn't perform offstage for the public, when producers like the great Charles Frohman believed that glamor was achieved through mystery. George C. Tyler, who did so much to develop me into a star during the years I was under contract to him, used to say, "A star should not be seen in public. The public will not pay to see on the stage a star it can see free in a restaurant." It was not unusual for a star of the stature of Maude Adams to refuse to be interviewed at all.

I don't know how it happened, but one day all of this changed and suddenly I was plunged into the world where an actor is public property. Of course, even in my youth he was, but only on the stage. Now his or her whole life is public property, and, as public property, I never have been comfortable. I never have known how to handle the situation. Besides, I never felt that I was very interesting as a celebrity off the stage. I remember once complaining to my husband, Charles MacArthur, about this. I said, "I know it's part of my job to be something more interesting than I am and I wish I knew what to do." And he said, "Well, you'll just have to write yourself a role for offstage and play it." To this I replied, "All right, you're the playwright, you write the role and I'll try to do it to the best of my ability." Well, we pondered over that role and then we both said, "Oh heck, let it go." I am what I am, and we agreed that it would be too wearisome and would take too much strength to play that offstage performance. Besides, I needed my concentration for my work in the theater.

Personally, I don't believe that in all my years I've known more than a few persons who enjoyed the obligations of fame, and even about them I may be wrong. For example,

I used to think that one of those who seemed to be most completely delighted by the adulation of the crowd was Joan Crawford. Some years ago when she was one of Hollywood's foremost stars, she was in New York for a visit, and she and I went to the theater together. Coming out, we were confronted by a mob. Joan blanched and said, "Oh God! I'm always so afraid they're going to say something to hurt me. I'm always trying to placate them. I'm always trying to keep them as my friends." How well I understood this fear. A mob can and will turn on you in a split second. They hurt me once very deeply. They turned on me and I was innocent. I've always tried to cooperate with them because they scare me to death. It was the closing night in Pittsburgh of the greatest success of my career—*Victoria Regina*. We had run for four and a half years in two different engagements, the second being a triumphant return to New York after two years on the road. And then we did another half season on tour. Everywhere we went was like a royal procession. Mayors met us at the station and we got the full treatment, red carpets and all. And don't think I didn't appreciate it and savor it. I was totally aware of what was happening to me. And I was also aware that it wasn't going to happen again because that sort of role and that sort of success never happen to an actress twice in her life. Why should I be the exception? When we reached Pittsburgh for the closing, word arrived that, although Gilbert Miller, the producer, would not be able to attend— I think he'd had to go to Europe—he had made arrangements for a champagne-and-caviar supper after the final curtain fell. All this was to take place on the stage, and an orchestra had been engaged to play "Auld Lang Syne" and, because there were so many English actors in the company, "God Save the King." All this was most thoughtful of

Gilbert, but I could share in only a minimum of the festivities. It had always been an agony for me to leave my husband and children at home when I had to go on tour, and now that it was about to be over I could hardly wait to get back to them. I found out that there was a midnight train from Pittsburgh that could get me home a few hours earlier than if I waited and took a morning plane. I was determined to be aboard that train. The company understood. After I had gotten out of my costume and changed, I went onto the stage, lifted the glass—one last toast to those actors with whom I had spent four and a half years—and then fled. Out in the alley there was quite a large crowd. They all swarmed around me, and I remember the company manager pleading, "Please, she has to make a train. She wants to get back to her family. Please don't stop Miss Hayes now." And I was pleading also, as we kept working our way to the car. We finally made it and I fell back against the seat in such relief. The car had to back out of the alley, which was very narrow, and the driver had to work with great caution. The crowd reluctantly spread and gave ground. But one voice began chanting—and it was taken up by many others until as we backed out of that alley and away from *Victoria Regina,* my greatest success, the words that I could hear were, "You stink! You stink! You stink!" Only because I had not stopped to sign my autograph. This is what scares you about the mob. It can spoil a lovely moment, and it can spoil your self-esteem.

We in the public eye know that this is one of the risks of fame. But what of those inspired people, the world's geniuses who have serious work to do on behalf of humanity? They are exposed, too. Jonas Salk, whose vaccine, thank God, helped turn the tide against the scourge of poliomyelitis, has said, "Fame is transitory, a waster. I'd rather stay in my laboratory and work." I have included in this section Clifton Fadiman's story of Madame Marie Curie, *She Didn't Know How To Be Famous.* She was one of those who had to suffer and struggle against the inroads of fame. I saw her once. I was twenty then, yet I have not forgotten that face.

It was after the First World War, and I was on the *S.S. Olympic,* making my first voyage abroad. Madame Curie was on that ship with her daughter. She had been to the United States, as Mr. Fadiman notes, for the purpose of receiving a gram of radium to take back to her laboratory. The schoolchildren of America had been asked to contribute to buying the radium as a gift from our country. Well, I hardly need stress the fact that everyone on that ship was not only excited and thrilled but also that some were just a little alarmed, that is, those who didn't exactly know what radium was and thought it might even blow up the ship.

Madame Curie was never seen except for a brief period before lunch or afterward when her daughter, holding her firmly by the arm, would haul her up on deck, walk her around three or four times, and then take her below deck again. Every day I would watch this performance, and my heart would bleed. The face was so beautiful, the head so lovely with its froth of white hair beneath a black skimmer. There was nothing of the world about that face. And everything about her—every detail—was burned into my mind. Held by her daughter as they walked around on deck, she looked to me like some fragile creature under arrest. And, in a sense she was—a hostage to her fame, and her daughter her jailer and bodyguard at the same time. If anyone made a compulsive move toward her, as tourists are wont to do, the daughter would shake her head to warn him off. When someone persisted, I remember my fury, my horror, my anxiety. Like that daughter, I felt I was a guardian over this exquisite, fragile creature who "didn't know how to be famous."

Years later for the final scene of the film *The Sin of Madelon Claudet,* which my husband wrote for me and for which I won an Oscar, I had to dress as an old woman. I wouldn't let anyone design my costume because I knew exactly what I would wear. I was going to look like Madame Curie, to recapture that image that had remained with me of a woman from whom all worldliness and earthliness had vanished, in whom nothing but the spiritual remained. And somehow, what I knew I wanted most was that black skimmer, that sort of sailor hat that seemed to enhance that spirituality. Everyone in the studio was horrified over the idea of the black skimmer. But Charlie took me to the costume department and we started rummaging, and there we found what I wanted—one of those Spanish dancer's hats with a big rose in it. "Take the rose off," I said, "and this is what I will wear." And because, when I play a role, I have to feel and see someone, all through the last part of *The Sin of Madelon Claudet* I thought of that picture I used to see on the deck of the *S.S. Olympic.* I hope Madame Curie forgives me.

SHE DID NOT KNOW HOW TO BE FAMOUS

Descartes was unheroic, Leibnitz a fawning courtier, Willard Gibbs a recluse, Gauss cold and secretive. For all his nobility, Pasteur was tainted with chauvinism and race hatred. A dubious religiosity clouded to the end the magnificent minds of Newton and Pascal. Indeed, it is hard to think of many first-rate scientific careers in which some major flaw of character does not show itself, confounding our natural desire for whole-hearted hero worship. But the lives of Marie and Pierre Curie, two of the most beautiful lives, I suppose, that have ever been lived, provided an exception. It was almost theatrically apt that this man and woman, with characters of shining purity, should have built their careers around a physical element recognizable by its indestructible and essential radiance.

The life of Marie Curie might have been conceived not by the accidents of nature but by the patterning brain of a tragic dramatist of genius.

One looks at a photograph of Marie taken in 1929, when she was sixty-two. The face is lined. From underneath the white and casually arranged hair arcs an abnormally spacious brow. She is dressed in a simple black dress that looks like a laboratory smock. The face is that of a truly beautiful woman, the beauty lying in the bones and in the brain that sends its clear signals through the deep, penetrating eyes.

The story of Marie Curie is not merely that of a poor Polish governess who struggled against adversity and became a triumphant success. The story of Marie Curie lies precisely in the fact that she was happiest during her struggles and least happy when a vulgar world acclaimed her. Hers is a success story with an ironic twist. Einstein has said, "Marie Curie is, of all celebrated beings, the only one whom fame has not corrupted." "She did not know how to be famous," says Eve Curie in her classic biography of her mother. In one deliberate sentence she strikes to the heart of the secret: "I hope that the reader may constantly feel, across the ephemeral movement of one existence, what in Marie Curie was even more rare than her work or her life: the immovable structure of a character; the stubborn effort of an intelligence; the free immolation of a human being that could give all and take nothing, could even receive nothing; and above all the quality of a soul in which neither fame nor adversity could change the exceptional purity."

Recall that unbelievably dramatic life. She is born Marja Sklodowska, youngest child of a Warsaw physicist and a sensitive, tubercular mother. The childhood is unhappy, torn by the death of mother and eldest sister, rendered overserious by poverty, given a certain tenseness by the fact that she is a member of a subject race, the Poles. She grows up, becomes the conventional intellectual rebel of her time, like "all the little Polish girls who had gone mad for culture." She is intelligent, but nothing yet reveals that "immovable structure" of which her daughter speaks. She becomes a governess, a bit of a bluestocking touched with Tolstoyan sentimentality. Now "the eternal student" begins to rise up in her. The little child who at five stood in rapt awe before her father's case containing the "phys-ics ap-pa-ra-tus" reawakens in the girl of eighteen. Her duties as a governess do not prevent her from studying. She has no money, not even for stamps so that she may write to her brother. But "I am learning chemistry from a book." Back in Warsaw, she is allowed to perform elementary chemical experiments in a real laboratory, and at last, after inconceivable setbacks and economies, after years of weary waiting, she goes to Paris to study at the Sorbonne.

On forty rubles a month Marja (now Marie) Sklodowska lives, studies, learns. Solitude, near-starvation, an unheated garret—none of these things matters, as long as at least a part of her day is spent in the laboratory. Now even the miserable forty rubles cease. She is about to return in despair to Warsaw when she is given a six-hundred-ruble scholarship. A few years afterward, with the first money she earns as a scientist, she returns the amount of the scholarship so that some other poor student may be assisted by it.

In 1894 she meets Pierre Curie, already a physicist of note, a mind "both powerful and noble." In an atmosphere of garrets and laboratories, these two, very grave and serious, conduct their love affair. They marry. On her wedding day, to the generous friend who wishes to give her a bridal dress, she writes, "I have no dress except the one I wear every day. If you are going to be kind enough to give me one, please let it be practical and dark so that I can put it on afterwards to go to the laboratory."

It is a perfect marriage, the marriage not merely of two people who love each other but, what is incomparably more interesting and important, of two great physicists who can help each other. It is Marie, attracted by the uranium researches of Becquerel, who starts herself and her husband on the long, tedious, glorious path at the end of which lies radium. They know that radium and polonium (named by Marie to commemorate her beloved native land), exist, but they must prove it. From 1898 to 1902, in a dilapidated, leaking, freezing shed, with primitive apparatus, with little or no help, unaided by the scientific bureaucracy or by the State, these two gentle fanatics work in an absorption that is like a dream. The government is too busy spending money on armament to buy them the few tons of pitchblende they need. Somehow they get their pitchblende, paying for its transportation themselves out of their insufficient salaries. With "her terrible patience," Marie, doing the work of four strong men, pounds away at her chemical masses, boils, separates, refines, stirs, strains. Somewhere in this inert brown stuff lies radium. Marie loses fifteen pounds during these five years. At last they isolate the element.

All this time they have been bringing up a family. They have had sorrows, family illnesses. Pierre's mother has died of the very disease against which radium is soon to prove a weapon. All this time no provision is made for these selfless geniuses. The State, as always, cares nothing. Recognition comes first from other countries, from Switzerland, England. "With great merit and even greater modesty," says Montaigne, "one can remain unknown for a long time."

Now the full implications of their work begin to appear. The immovable atom moves; matter is touched with a mysterious life; physics revises its nineteenth-century conceptions of the indestructibility of matter and the conservation of energy. The Curies are triumphant; and their first major decision is to refrain from patenting their radium-extraction process. They give it freely to the world. This gesture alone is enough to lend their lives a depth that can never attach to a career like that of Edison. The difference between a Curie and an Edison is not merely one of scientific genius, it is a difference of order. The Curies are one kind of human being, Edison was another.

In 1903 the Curies, with Becquerel, receive the Nobel Prize for Physics. The world pursues them. Now they must flee the world. "In science we must be interested in things, not persons," says Marie, who was never to be interested in herself. One evening, at the height of their fame, as they are about to leave for a banquet, Pierre looks at his wife, with her ash-gray eyes, her ash-blond hair, her exquisite wrists and ankles, and he murmurs, "It's a pity. Evening dress becomes you." Then, with a sigh, he adds, "But there it is, we haven't got time."

They are offered the slimy vulgarity of decorations, ribbons, rosettes. But no laboratory. Pierre died without getting his laboratory.

Then on April 19, 1906, Aeschylean tragedy, cutting

Marie's life in two, giving it at the same time a new emotional dimension. Pierre's head is crushed by a van in a street accident, and Marie becomes "a pitiful and incurably lonely woman." She refuses a pension (always the State makes its generous offers too late); she proceeds with the education of her daughters; she takes over Pierre's teaching post and, in a dry, monotonous voice, without making any reference to her predecessor, resumes the lectures at the exact point at which Pierre had left off.

The rest of her life is the story of her marriage with radium. For her laboratory, for science, she will do anything, even try to be "famous." In 1911 she receives the Nobel Prize for Chemistry. During the war she equips, with superhuman energy, a fleet of radiological cars so that the wounded may be helped by X-rays. She is no rotogravure ministering angel, no Queen Marie of Rumania. She actually works—works for the State which had done its best in those dark years to prevent her from working. Later, again for the sake of science, she comes to America to receive a gram of radium from the hand of an amiable poker player who could not possibly have understood even the most trivial of the thoughts in Marie Curie's mind. Then, applauded by all America, she goes back to France, and all America turns to the next celebrity, Carpentier, to lavish an identical adulation upon him. Almost blind, her hands and arms scarred, pitted, and burned by thirty years of radium emanations, she continues her work almost to the day of her death, caused in part by that very element which she had released for the use of mankind.

CLIFTON FADIMAN

I THINK CONTINUALLY OF THOSE

I think continually of those who were truly great.
Who, from the womb, remembered the soul's history
Through corridors of light where the hours are suns,
Endless and singing. Whose lovely ambition
Was that their lips, still touched with fire,
Should tell of the spirit clothed from head to foot in
    song.
And who hoarded from the spring branches
The desires falling across their bodies like blossoms.

What is precious is never to forget
The essential delight of the blood drawn from ageless
    springs
Breaking through rocks in worlds before our earth.
Never to deny its pleasure in the simple morning light
Nor its grave evening demand for love.
Never to allow gradually the traffic to smother
With noise and fog the flowering of the spirit.

Near the snow, near the sun, in the highest fields
See how these names are fêted by the waving grass,
And by the streamers of white cloud,
And whispers of wind in the listening sky;
The names of those who in their lives fought for life,
Who wore at their hearts the fire's center.
Born of the sun they traveled a short while towards the
    sun,
And left the vivid air signed with their honor.

STEPHEN SPENDER

WHEN I HAVE FEARS THAT I MAY CEASE TO BE

When I have fears that I may cease to be
Before my pen has gleaned my teeming brain,
Before high-pilèd books, in charact'ry
Hold like rich garners the full-ripened grain;
When I behold, upon the night's starred face,
Huge cloudy symbols of a high romance,
And think that I may never live to trace
Their shadows, with the magic hand of chance;
And when I feel, fair creature of an hour!
That I shall never look upon thee more,
Never have relish in the fairy power
Of unreflecting love!—then on the shore
  Of the wide world I stand alone, and think
  Till Love and Fame to nothingness do sink.

JOHN KEATS

From THE SUMMING UP

But the greatest danger that besets the professional author is one that unfortunately only a few have to guard against. Success. It is the most difficult thing the writer has to cope with. When after a long and bitter struggle he has at last achieved it he finds that it spreads a snare to entangle and destroy him. Few of us have the determination to avoid its perils. It must be dealt with warily. The common idea that success spoils people by making them vain, egotistic and self-complacent is erroneous; on the contrary it makes them, for the most part, humble, tolerant and kind. Failure makes people bitter and cruel. Success improves the character of the man; it does not always improve the character of the author.

W. SOMERSET MAUGHAM

Priscilla Ives was my maid. She said this to me when she visited me in the hospital in 1941. I was recuperating from an operation for acute bursitis. I had been trying to work our farm all day and play in *Harriet* at night—and I had brought on that painful ailment in my shoulder.

Miss Hayes, I think the good Lord knows what he's doing. I believe he intended some people to be farmers like Mr. Dyer and some people to be maids like me and some people to be actresses like you, but he never, in all this world, intended anybody to be an actress and a farmer too.

Walking

I NOTICED in a magazine article that walking may be on
the way back. In fact, by the time this reaches print
it may already be "in." Which, I know, will lift a heavy
burden from a lot of good souls who have almost begun to
feel like members of some outlawed sect. In this age of the
motorcar when Johnny not only can't read but also can't
fetch the Sunday newspaper without the family car—a junket
all of two blocks' distance—some of us have become rather
defensive about our predilection for walking. We have had
to learn to weather the astonished expressions of our friends,
not to mention those politely raised eyebrows that ineffec-
tually try to hide the thought that we are somewhat tetched.
Even the golf course, that green haven of walkers, is being
overrun by electric-powered carts carrying men and women
from tee to fairway to rough to putting green.

I'm a walker from away back. Not perhaps as ardent as
say Harry Truman or that Manhattan crowd that considers
it a day ill-spent that does not include several brisk turns

around the reservoir in Central Park. But I am loyal to the creed. Loyal enough, for example, to defy convention even in Cuernavaca, Mexico. When I first bought my house in Cuernavaca, I alarmed many of my North American friends, and particularly my sister-in-law, Mary MacArthur, who had persuaded me to establish a residence there, by my devotion to walking. They explained to me that I was a great personage of the theater, that I had been expected to bring a certain dignity and glamor to the place and instead I was being seen all over, walking up and down the streets, poking into the alleys and squares, shopping in the marketplace and the stores—and, worst of all, carrying my bundles home in my own arms. Finally, my sister-in-law, driven frantic by her consternation over my behavior, took me aside one day and said, "Helen, you just can't do this. You simply can't. You can do this back home in Nyack and be safe. But here— the Mexicans will not respect you if you walk back and forth carrying bundles." I listened as patiently as I could. "You must understand," she went on, "that ladies in Latin American countries simply don't walk and carry things. You must at least have a little boy carry the bundles behind you."

When Mary had said that ladies in Latin America didn't walk, there flashed through my mind a luncheon I'd had many years ago in the Copley Plaza Hotel in Boston with the novelist Mary Roberts Rinehart. (I was then appearing in *Bab*, which Edward Childs Carpenter had adapted from Mrs. Rinehart's famous stories about the Boston sub-deb.) When she lit a cigarette, a maître d' came over to the table and said, "I'm so sorry, madame, but ladies are not permitted to smoke here." And she looked at him with a kind of helpful smile and said, "But I'm not a lady," and went on smoking.

So, when my sister-in-law said ladies in Latin American countries do not walk, I just said, "Oh Mary, there's no use.

You can't make a silk purse out of that well-known other thing and I'm just not a lady and you're not going to make me into one. I'll give a little boy a few pesos to carry the bundles, but I'll continue to walk."

Walking has made me a terrible pest to some people. Once, when my husband was still alive, and we were abroad, I went to the Firth of Clyde in Scotland with him and an English friend, Bobby Throckmorton, to see Lord Inverclyde in his castle there. These were witty men—Charlie and Bobby—and Inverclyde was no slouch either. They just wanted to sit around and jabber and have a good time, but I wanted to walk a moor. So after a day or so of listening to me wanting to walk a moor, they loaded me into Inverclyde's Rolls Royce, and these three stalwart men drove little me up to the edge of a moor and dumped me there and rode away to sit in the village pub and enjoy a beer.

I feel sorry now for members of the companies with which I used to tour. In those days when I really was famous I didn't have the nerve to walk around the streets alone for fear of being bothered and robbed of the relaxation I was seeking. So friends would escort me on my wanderings. When I was on tour in *Victoria Regina* everyone treated me offstage as though I were still a queen. They behaved like courtiers trying to keep me happy. But I learned after a while, after I had worn out several good friends, that the cast had met in solemn conclave to parcel me out: "You walk her Tuesday, and I'll walk her Wednesday."

I believe it was my mother who really was responsible for my addiction to walking. Mother and I left Washington, D.C., when I was nine years old to come to New York so that I could get started on a career in the theater. I got my first job with Lew Fields in *Old Dutch* (an operetta by Victor Herbert—perhaps his *only* failure) and remained with him for several seasons, appearing in three subsequent productions. We went out on tour after the New York runs, and this was a real adventure for mother and me. She was free from household chores and was enjoying every minute of it. We walked everywhere, mostly because we didn't know how to get where we were going any other way, and we certainly couldn't afford taxis.

In addition to mother, there was another influence on my walking. That was John Drew, with whom I appeared in *The Prodigal Husband* when I was fourteen. When we went on tour, Drew would take me on long walks all over the city in which we were playing. He said it was part of my education and it would help broaden my perspective on my country. So when we went to Cambridge, Massachusetts, we walked all over Cambridge, and when we played in Buffalo, he'd take mother and me to the Falls and we'd walk around there. And that's what I do now, automatically. I just walk everywhere. It's habit. No matter where I am I walk. I have an insatiable inquisitiveness. I'm greedy for sights and sounds, and sometimes I even frighten people. Not so long ago I went on a trip to Egypt to see the pyramids, and everyone was terribly concerned because before we had started I injured my back. But I insisted on walking wherever we were, walking like a crazy woman, wanting not to miss a thing. I think you miss so much of a city when you just drive around. You must walk to get the feel, to be able to remember what you saw. It is only when I've walked around a place—stopped and studied and imagined—that I can close my eyes and return myself, at least in spirit, to where I was. Even in familiar places there are always new things to be seen. As Brooks Atkinson has said, "To walk is to be free. It is escape from the system of telephones, subways, office and routine; and it is foreign travel only a few blocks from home."

When I was in Ireland, I spent one day being driven around the bogs in a jaunting car—a two-wheeled vehicle with seats placed lengthwise back to back and extending over the wheels. There were four persons in the car besides the driver, who had a small seat in front. The place was very Irish and full of mysticism, and the combination got the better of me. As my companions were pointing out the bogs and telling me how people would jump from one hummock to the other, I suddenly announced, "Listen, I come from a long line of bog-jumpers and I cannot stand it that I am sitting in this car being toted through this place." So the driver stopped, and I got out and did my happy bog-jumping by myself, meeting up with the car later at the crossroads. It seems that you have to fight these days for a chance to feel good earth under your feet.

My first travels in Europe were made under the guidance of one who had known Europe "when." That is, before world wars and tourist rates. Tourism was yet to be born, and foreign travel belonged exclusively to the intellectuals and high society. I shall always wince at the recollection of that trip in 1921. I was so young and palpitating with eagerness and mother had saved so hard to make this exposure to Culture possible. And then our self-appointed guide, producer George C. Tyler, very nearly ruined it all. From the minute he met us at Cherbourg and started the drive to Paris, he complained. Complained of the altered face of the landscape, complained of the degeneration of the cuisine, of the service, of the crowds, of just about everything. And for all of it he held the new rush of tourists responsible. After a week of this, I made a decision. I was going to enjoy this trip and the many I hoped would follow *because* of and not in *spite* of my fellow-tourists. I have kept that pact with myself ever since and have been a very happy sight-seer. When I want solitude, I go for a walk in the woods. When I go to see places, I like to encounter them as they were meant to be when they were built—that is, throbbing with life, teeming with people, with noise and excitement. It took me a while to break myself of disdain for guides, but now I quite like them, lies and all. As Walt Whitman said,

> There is something in staying close to men and women
>   and looking on them, and in the contact and odor
>   of them, that pleases the soul well,
> All things please the soul, but these please the soul well.

One of my favorite walks, when I'm home in Nyack, is on the path along the Hudson River leading to Hook Mountain, that mysterious and wonderful-looking mountain with a bite out of its side where once were the quarries that supplied the brownstone for so many fashionable houses in New York. From my house on North Broadway it is about three miles up and back. And though I have done it for years—there were times when I did it every day—I have never tired of it. There seems always to be something new to watch on the river, something new to marvel at in the thickets and the woods. I usually have one or two of my French poodles with me on my walk, and with their support I am brave. I prowl and poke my nose into odd places; occasionally I dart into what was once an estate and now stands deserted. There have been many wonderful moments on these walks, such as the time I passed through a tall overgrown hedge and came out on the other side flushing

a great flock of wild canaries. They flew in a swarm around
me and then away.

On days when I am especially ambitious, I will follow
the path beyond Hook Mountain and head to a point farther
up, opposite Ossining, before turning around for home. But
it makes little difference to me really whether I'm on my
way to Hook Mountain and beyond or hiking down Fifth
Avenue—everywhere I am witness to the greatest shows on
earth.

From WALKING

I think that I cannot preserve my health and spirits
unless I spend four hours a day at least—and it is commonly more than that—sauntering through the woods
and over the hills and fields, absolutely free from all
worldly engagements. You may safely say, A penny for
your thoughts, or a thousand pounds. When sometimes
I am reminded that the mechanics and shopkeepers stay
in their shops not only all the forenoon, but all the
afternoon too, sitting with crossed legs, so many of them
—as if the legs were made to sit upon, and not to stand
or walk upon—I think that they deserve some credit
for not having all committed suicide long ago.

No doubt temperament and, above all, age have a
good deal to do with it. As a man grows older, his ability
to sit still and follow indoor occupations increases. He
grows vespertinal in his habits as the evening of life
approaches, till at last he comes forth only just before
sundown and gets all the walk that he requires in half
an hour.

But the walking of which I speak has nothing in it
akin to taking exercise, but is itself the enterprise and
adventure of the day. If you would get exercise, go in

search of the springs of life. Think of a man's swinging dumbbells for his health, when those springs are
bubbling up in far-off pastures unsought by him!

Moreover, you must walk like a camel, which is said
to be the only beast which ruminates when walking.
When a traveler asked Wordsworth's servant to show
him her master's study, she answered, "Here is his
library, but his study is out of doors."

HENRY DAVID THOREAU

From SPEED

The other day, a motoristic friend of mine was complaining to me bitterly, even violently, about the be-
haviour of pedestrians. They were abominably careless
and stupid, he insisted. I hate to see anyone agitated
by a grievance, and I tried to soothe my friend by an
appeal to reason. I said, "No doubt we pedestrians are
very trying. But you must remember that, after all, we
were on the roads for many, many centuries before
you came along in your splendid car. And remember,
it isn't we that are threatening to kill *you*. It is you that
are threatening to kill *us*. And if we are rather flustered,
and occasionally do the wrong thing, you should make
allowances—and, if the worst comes to the worst, lay
some flowers on our graves."

MAX BEERBOHM

TO A YOUNG LADY WHO HAD BEEN
REPROACHED FOR TAKING LONG WALKS
IN THE COUNTRY

Dear child of Nature, let them rail!
—There is a next in a green dale,

A harbor and a hold;
Where thou, a Wife and Friend, shalt see
Thy own heart-stirring days, and be
A light to young and old.

There, healthy as a shepherd boy,
And treading among flowers of joy
Which at no season fade,
Thou, while thy babes around thee cling,
Shalt show us how divine a thing
A Woman may be made.

Thy thoughts and feelings shall not die,
Nor leave thee, when gray hairs are nigh,
A melancholy slave;
But an old age serene and bright,
And lovely as a Lapland night,
Shall lead thee to thy grave.

WILLIAM WORDSWORTH

TRAVEL

I should like to rise and go
Where the golden apples grow;
Where below another sky
Parrot islands anchored lie,
And, watched by cockatoos and goats,
Lonely Crusoes building boats;
Where in sunshine reaching out
Eastern cities, miles about,
Are with mosque and minaret
Among sandy gardens set,
And the rich goods from near and far
Hang for sale in the bazaar;

Where the Great Wall round China goes,
And on one side the desert blows,
And with bell and voice and drum,
Cities on the other hum;
Where are forests, hot as fire,
Wide as England, tall as a spire,
Full of apes and coco-nuts
And the negro hunters' huts;
Where the knotty crocodile
Lies and blinks in the Nile,
And the red flamingo flies
Hunting fish before his eyes;
Where in jungles, near and far,
Man-devouring tigers are,
Lying close and giving ear
Lest the hunt be drawing near,
Or a comer-by be seen
Swinging in a palanquin;
Where among the desert sands
Some deserted city stands,
All its children, sweep and prince,
Grown to manhood ages since,
Not a foot in street or house,
Not a stir of child or mouse,
And when kindly falls the night,
In all the town no spark of light.
There I'll come when I'm a man
With a camel caravan;
Light a fire in the gloom
Of some dusty dining-room;
See the pictures on the walls,
Heroes, fights and festivals;
And in a corner find the toys
Of the old Egyptian boys.

ROBERT LOUIS STEVENSON

From THE MEANING OF PLACE

I confess that I never respond to places like the Colosseum, or Pompeii, or the Roman Forum, or the ruins of Ostia or Agrigento, unless my imagination, or some learned and sensitive friend, can first people them for me as they were when they were alive. (It is characteristic of the sentimental delusion that Stendhal felt that the Colosseum is much more impressive now as a ruin than it ever was when it was in actual use. Then, he says, it was only a theatre. "Only" a theatre!)

Indeed the only time I am certain that I am getting the true feel of Rome itself is when I am, let us say, sitting chatting with some dear friend in the Pincio Gardens, watching the lovers and the children and the idlers stroll by; or lunching after on the terrace of the Villa Valadier overlooking Rome's level plain of roofs, and towers and domes, seeing it all as one close weave of present and past, one unity in which the old Rome was not something secluded or insulated from the new but a continuing and creative power that held, and foretold, and compelled the lovers, the children and the idlers, and the Frascati shining on my table, and even me privileged to share one exquisite moment of its unbroken continuum.

This is why I distrust travelers who dislike change and clamor for the preservation of things as they were when they first saw them. I distrust their life-sense. I feel they are interested less in men than in monuments. Carcassonne has been "preserved" stone by stone with loving devotion; it is literally stone-dead. Bruges is a stuffed bird. Weimar may be found touching by moonlight; it does not survive the busy, human morning. But Ravenna, where only the mosaics are tended, is palpitating with the happy come-and-go of present life.

That splendidly neglected town of Aigues-Mortes, south of Nîmes, once a port, now abandoned by the tide, is attractive not for its age but as a pleasant oasis of present-day Provençal life.

Where past and present mingle like this, enriching one another, informing one another, we have the best of both worlds. Paris and Rome are the royal examples. One can, to be sure, be sentimental in Paris, go about taking photographs of "picturesque bits"; but not for long. In Rome even Stendhal occasionally came to the surface; as when, unguardedly, forgetting fashion, he admitted that the ideal time to appraise the Colosseum is "after midnight, with an attractive woman."

It is one of the most difficult things in the world to be natural. There is always some fashionable way of seeing and feeling. The modern fashion is the Social Conscience, which is infinitely more boring than the Sentimental Eye. The number of young Americans I have talked to in Europe who see nothing at all but statistics, underemployment, bad finance, political chaos, moral turpitude, under-production and the devil knows what other social abstraction! The only possible thing to say to these sad young people is that the best way to see any city at all is "after midnight, with an attractive young woman"—and then, by Heaven, I swear they would sit in the Colosseum reading a Senate report by the light of the moon.

SEAN O'FAOLAIN

In 1945 I was rehearsing *The Glass Menagerie* in London, under John Gielgud's direction. I lived in Bea Lillie's flat on Park Lane and walked to the Haymarket Theatre every day, and home again by a different route till I had exhausted all the ways; then I went back to repeat my favorites. After a couple of weeks, I walked once each day along Grosvenor Street to pause and mourn before a lovely old house there. Its entire front had been blown away, leaving it with the appearance of a great doll's house, with all its rooms exposed to the prying sun and rain. On the second floor was an exquisitely paneled room with carved garlands that might have been Grinling Gibbons'. A community of pigeons lived there —such filthy tenants.

Ten years later, on a return trip to London, I made straight for Grosvenor Street, and there was my house, its façade restored, mellowed, distinguished.

From STREET HAUNTING

A London Adventure

No one perhaps has ever felt passionately towards a lead pencil. But there are circumstances in which it can become supremely desirable to possess one; moments when we are set upon having an object, an excuse for walking half across London between tea and dinner. As the foxhunter hunts in order to preserve the breed of foxes, and the golfer plays in order that open spaces may be preserved from the builders, so when the desire comes upon us to go street rambling a pencil does for a pretext, and getting up we say: "Really I must buy a pencil," as if under cover of this excuse we could indulge safely in the greatest pleasure of town life in winter—rambling the streets of London.

The hour should be the evening and the season winter, for in winter the champagne brightness of the air and the sociability of the streets are grateful. We are not then haunted as in the summer by the longing for shade and solitude and sweet airs from the hayfields. The evening hour, too, gives us the irresponsibility which darkness and lamplight bestow. We are no longer quite ourselves. As we step out of the house on a fine evening between four and six, we shed the self our friends know us by and become part of that vast republican army of anonymous trampers, whose society is so agreeable after the solitude of one's own room. For there we sit surrounded by objects which perpetually express the oddity of our own temperaments and enforce the memories of our experience. That bowl on the mantelpiece, for instance, was bought at Mantua on a windy day. We were leaving the shop when the sinister old woman plucked at our skirts and said she would find herself starving one of these days, but, "Take it!" she cried, and thrust the blue and white china bowl into our hands as if she never wanted to be reminded of her quixotic generosity. So, guiltily, but suspecting nevertheless how badly we had been fleeced, we carried it back to the little hotel where, in the middle of the night, the innkeeper quarrelled so violently with his wife that we all leant out into the courtyard to look, and saw the vines laced among the pillars and the stars white in the sky. The moment was stabilized, stamped like a coin indelibly among a million that slipped by imperceptibly. There, too, was the melancholy Englishman, who rose among the coffee cups and the little iron tables and revealed the secrets of his soul—as travellers do. All this— Italy, the windy morning, the vines laced about the pillars, the Englishman and the secrets of his soul—rise up in a cloud from the china bowl on the mantelpiece. And there, as our eyes fall to the floor, is that brown stain on the carpet. Mr. Lloyd George made that. "The man's a devil!" said Mr. Cummings, putting the kettle down with which he was about to fill the teapot so that it burnt a brown ring on the carpet.

But when the door shuts on us, all that vanishes. The

shell-like covering which our souls have excreted to house themselves, to make for themselves a shape distinct from others, is broken, and there is left of all these wrinkles and roughness a central oyster of perceptiveness, an enormous eye. How beautiful a street is in winter! It is at once revealed and obscured. Here vaguely one can trace symmetrical straight avenues of doors and windows; here under the lamps are floating islands of pale light through which pass quickly bright men and women, who, for all their poverty and shabbiness, wear a certain look of unreality, an air of triumph, as if they had given life the slip, so that life, deceived of her prey, blunders on without them. But, after all, we are only gliding smoothly on the surface. The eye is not a miner, not a diver, not a seeker after buried treasure. It floats us smoothly down a stream; resting, pausing, the brain sleeps perhaps as it looks.

How beautiful a London street is then, with its islands of light, and its long groves of darkness, and on one side of it perhaps some tree-sprinkled, grass-grown space where night is folding herself to sleep naturally and, as one passes the iron railing, one hears those little cracklings and stirrings of leaf and twig which seem to suppose the silence of fields all round them, an owl hooting, and far away the rattle of a train in the valley.

VIRGINIA WOOLF

Shakespeare

I'VE always been grateful that I was fortunate enough to have been introduced to Shakespeare's sonnets outside the bleak atmosphere of the schoolroom, although I had had some experience with the mill and the sausage machine—the academic approach that places such rigidity and constraint upon the young mind in learning Shakespeare.

I was given, when I was a small child, Charles and Mary Lamb's *Tales from Shakespeare*. These I loved. The stories and their eloquent descriptions of the people, and the wonderful things that happened, were exciting to my child's imagination. But then when I got into the upper grades during my few darts into school between professional engagements in the theater, I was exposed to that awful bookish Shakespeare where you are set to learning twenty lines a night and you don't care what the lines are about just so long as you get them into your head and get your grade. I remember also those horrible little gray volumes—

and they were literally gray—with every line numbered, and those horrid little head-crushing notes at the bottom. It all was like having an autopsy in the classroom every day, and that tremulous beautiful thing that was there on the pages turned into a corpse for the bored students. Ghastly. I don't even like to think about it now. For years, until I read them on my own, *A Midsummer Night's Dream, The Merchant of Venice*, and even the soul-shaking *Hamlet* lay dead in my head.

I am not an educator, but I often wish that there was some way for youngsters to discover Shakespeare for themselves, as I did the sonnets. I had been told to read them because of my diction, not because they were good for me. Although I was by then familiar with the plays, the sonnets were new to me. And I came to love them.

It happened when I was nineteen and I was in rehearsal for James M. Barrie's *Dear Brutus*. Charles Frohman had hired me to play the role of Margaret opposite William Gillette and he assigned B. Iden Payne as the director. Mr. Payne was an Englishman who later was to become the head of the drama department at the Carnegie Institute of Technology. During the third or fourth rehearsal Mr. Payne came down to the footlights and said, looking straight at me, "I want to talk to that little girl." My heart jumped into my throat as he went on. "I don't understand," he said. "You have a strange accent or manner of speech that I don't understand and I don't know that it fits into this role." I stood there frozen with horror, suspecting that the job was slipping from my grasp. Out, I thought, here I go, out. Mr. Payne went on with a long dissertation about my speech and his puzzlement over it when that gallant Mr. Gillette came to my rescue. He said, "This child has a Southern accent, and you aren't familiar with our accents in this country. She has a slight Southern accent. That's what it is and we can get her over that. I'll work with her evenings and we'll get her over it." Mr. Payne clearly didn't like the idea of Mr. Gillette working with me. He wanted to be in full control of the play. So he suggested to me that at home, in the evenings, I read aloud. He said, "Just choose anything at random. For instance, take the sonnets of Shakespeare and read them aloud and be sure that you sound your "d's" and cross your "t's" and get that curious "o" into what the English language intended it to be."

My "o," it is true, was a little bit like Eliza Doolittle's—a sort of "ow," that Southern "ow." I dashed from the rehearsal to the nearest bookstore, got the sonnets, and went home to read them. I didn't think about Shakespeare or how the very name struck awe in so many hearts. But before I had gone through three or four nights of reading the sonnets aloud I was caught up in them. He had come through and taken me over, Mr. Shakespeare, and what he was saying and the way he was saying it were so overwhelmingly wonderful that I had a hard time keeping my mind on those "d's," "t's," and that "o." Somehow, of course, I did manage to improve my diction and hold on to my job. But I held on to something more. There was created in me an appetite for the sonnets that would endure for the rest of my life. There aren't any that I do not know by now, some of them by heart. They are so utterly beautiful and so full of love.

I think that every woman can find the portrait of her lover in the sonnets, and I suppose every man can find that of his. For me, for example, there is the one in which I can see my Charlie when he was young. It is a very humorous one and it always reminds me of the lovely sort of teasing way with which Charlie approached our love. He would never be serious about it. He never wallowed about. That Charlie is in the 130th:

> My mistress' eyes are nothing like the sun;
> Coral is far more red than her lips' red;
> If snow be white, why then her breasts are dun;
> If hairs be wires, black wires grow on her head.
> I have seen roses damask'd, red and white,
> But no such roses see I in her cheeks;
> And in some perfumes is there more delight
> Than in the breath that from my mistress reeks.
> I love to hear her speak; yet well I know
> That music hath a far more pleasing sound.
> I grant I never saw a goddess go:
> My mistress, when she walks, treads on the ground.
>   And yet, by heaven, I think my love as rare
>   As any she belied with false compare.

There is another Charlie tucked away in the sonnets, the Charlie I remember in the last six years of his life, after he had lost Mary and his will to live.

People kept handing me roles to play so that I could take my battered spirits to the theater and somehow renew and heal them in the work. But I hadn't wanted to go on in the theater after that—I had lost my appetite for work anyway. I had this terrible self-consciousness about people looking at me and saying, "Oh, it's too bad, she's had a tragedy" and feeling sorry for me. I was oppressed by the horrid thought that they would be kind about my performance because they couldn't bear to hurt me again in any way. Besides, I wanted to be home with Charlie. I knew from the start that he was going to have to stare at an empty piece of paper in a typewriter and find something to put on it. And it's hard

to find something to put on it when there isn't anything left
in your mind or your heart but despair. But it was Charlie
who was always encouraging me, urging me to go back to
work. That was the Charlie of the 37th sonnet:

> As a decrepit father takes delight
> To see his active child do deeds of youth,
> So I, made lame by fortune's dearest spite,
> Take all my comfort of thy worth and truth;
> For whether beauty, birth, or wealth, or wit,
> Or any of these all, or all, or more,
> Entitled in thy parts do crowned sit,
> I make my love engrafted to this store.
> So then I am not lame, poor, nor despis'd,
> Whilst that this shadow doth such substance give
> That I in thy abundance am suffic'd
> And by a part of all thy glory live.
> > Look, what is best—that best I wish in thee.
> > This wish I have; then ten times happy me!

Among my favorites also is the 33rd:

> Full many a glorious morning have I seen
> Flatter the mountain tops with sovereign eye,
> Kissing with golden face the meadows green,
> Gilding pale streams with heavenly alchemy;
> Anon permit the basest clouds to ride
> With ugly rack on his celestial face
> And from the forlorn world his visage hide,
> Stealing unseen to West with this disgrace.
> Even so my sun one early morn did shine
> With all-triumphant splendour on my brow;
> But, out, alack! he was but one hour mine,
> The region cloud hath mask'd him from me now.
> > Yet him for this my love no whit disdaineth;

Suns of the world may stain when heaven's sun
   staineth.

Also the 116th:

Let me not to the marriage of true minds
Admit impediments. Love is not love
Which alters when it alteration finds
Or bends with the remover to remove.
O, no! it is an ever-fixed mark,
That looks on tempests and is never shaken;
It is the star to every wand'ring bark,
Whose worth's unknown, although his highth be taken.
Love's not Time's fool, though rosy lips and cheeks
Within his bending sickle's compass come.
Love alters not with his brief hours and weeks,
But bears it out even to the edge of doom.
   If this be error and upon me proved,
   I never writ, nor no man ever loved.

Now, let me recall how I found my very special favorite.
Shortly after my introduction to the sonnets themselves and
following the opening of *Dear Brutus*, I had gone to one of
those Sunday night Actors' Fund benefits. A Being walked
out on the stage that seemed to me to be the epitome of all
beauty and glamor—the magnificent Julia Marlowe, who
had begun her career in a juvenile *H.M.S. Pinafore* company
and had gone on to become one of the finest actresses in
Shakespearean roles. She came on the stage that night and
she had a little book in her hand. She stood in the middle
of the stage, raised her head and began to recite "Shall I
compare thee to a summer's day?" The lines, of course, were
those of the 18th sonnet, and I was hypnotized. That's what
Julia Marlowe could do. She could hypnotize people, and I

think that whatever sonnet she had chosen to read that night would have become my very special favorite. In fact, it probably was that night that the realization was born in me of the terrible power an actor has to sway people with a trick of personality, of voice, even of physical appearance. If what he says with his voice, if what he does with himself on a stage can have such an effect on people, then it is indeed a terrible power.

So herewith the 18th sonnet, along with the 19th, of which I am also deeply fond. Although not much heed generally is paid to it, the 19th is a continuation that rounds out the thought of the 18th.

Shall I compare thee to a summer's day?
Thou art more lovely and more temperate.
Rough winds do shake the darling buds of May,
And summer's lease hath all too short a date.
Sometime too hot the eye of heaven shines,
And often is his gold complexion dimm'd;
And every fair from fair sometime declines,
By chance or nature's changing course, untrimm'd;
But thy eternal summer shall not fade
Nor lose possession of that fair thou ow'st,
Nor shall Death brag thou wand'rest in his shade
When in eternal lines to time thou grow'st.
   So long as men can breathe, or eyes can see,
   So long lives this, and this gives life to thee.

Devouring Time, blunt thou the lion's paws
And make the earth devour her own sweet brood;
Pluck the keen teeth from the fierce tiger's jaws
And burn the long-liv'd phoenix in her blood;
Make glad and sorry seasons as thou fleets,
And do whate'er thou wilt, swift-footed Time,
To the wide world and all her fading sweets;

But I forbid thee one most heinous crime:
O, carve not with thy hours my love's fair brow,
Nor draw no lines there with thine antique pen!
Him in thy course untainted do allow
For beauty's pattern to succeeding men.
　　Yet do thy worst, old Time! Despite thy wrong,
　　My love shall in my verse ever live young.

I'm sure that there have been many changes in the study of Shakespeare in the schools, and I can only applaud the many wonderful efforts that are being made now in the theater and by educators to help make Shakespeare come alive through first-rate professional performances for school children by such fine organizations as the American Shakespeare Festival of Stratford, Conn., Lyn Ely's Theater in Education programs, The New York Shakespeare Festival, and others. But I am also afraid that more of this is needed, much more. From what I have observed and from what I have heard, too much of the old head-crushing system still prevails across our country. And what a shame! Shakespeare not only is a cornerstone of our culture, but more important to me is that he lives and breathes today as much as he did in Queen Elizabeth's day. How many insights he provides into the human brain and the human soul! He puts everything that is lost within us into the right words, crystallizes and brings into focus everything that we think and feel as human beings. What a joy it is, when we are going through some deep experience in our lives about which we are helplessly unable to articulate our feelings, to find these feelings perfectly expressed for us by Shakespeare. Wit, imagery, nature, and the flowers in our gardens, the trees along our roads and in the forests, the baser and nobler instincts of men and women—they are all there for us to enjoy and revel in. What a waste not to have access to them because the doors were closed by stuffy pedants intent on performing their autopsies.

But it isn't only the pedants who upset me. I also get irritated by all those tamperers who try to stretch Shakespeare this way and that, putting him into modern dress, shifting him here and there, all over the universe. I like my Shakespeare straight. I am sick and tired of everybody imposing his own smaller talent upon the much greater talent he is interpreting, of trying to put his own stamp on what someone else has created.

Naturally, I love all the big moments in Shakespeare, all the big passages that the world knows and loves. But the selections that follow are my own special secret joys.

When I was at the age when most of my school friends in Washington, D.C., were concentrating on dates and proms at Annapolis, I was touring the one-night-stand route through the Western and Southern states in a play called *Pollyanna, the Glad Girl.* That character was unquestionably the most obnoxious I have ever been called upon to play. The horrid little creature had invented the Glad Game. One had to find a reason to be glad for everything. Playing her eight times a week might have made a misanthrope out of me.

Our troupe consisted of some tired character actors who had about reached the end of the road and one wan, rather too blond young actor with whom I promptly fell in love, there being no one else handy. It was apparent early in the tour that none of these fellow-travelers would have the heart to cope with a bouncy seventeen-year-old who wanted to see and touch everything.

It might have been a lonely experience had it not been that one actor from England, George Allison, got me to read Shakespeare's plays. Shakespeare served as a good antidote to Pollyanna, and his people soon became very real and good friends. So eager was I to get back to the hotel and the next bloody murder in *Macbeth*, that there were whole performances when I was barely aware of what I was saying—lines like "I'm glad my legs are broken—glad, glad, GLAD!"

And so I took refuge in Shakespeare. And it amused me, during that lonely time, to build, out of bits and pieces of his heroines, an ideal woman to whom I could turn for inspiration and guidance. I took certain liberties, abridging and editing speeches, running lines from two different speeches together. But finally my fragments of Shakespeare ladies became one woman in all her varied colors and lights, in all her joys and griefs. And my one woman was really all women. Allow me to introduce her in her several aspects. If there is a preoccupation with romantic love in these passages I chose those many years ago, blame it on my youth.

First is Rosalind—like every girl who ever suffered the comic-sweet tortures of first love. Yearning, yet afraid of being hurt, she says, "Ominous, he comes to kill my heart!" She tries to shield that vulnerable heart with sophisticated words: "Men have died from time to time and worms have eaten them—but not for love." How she frets—even as you and I:

"Men are April when they woo, December when they wed. Maids are May when they are maids, but the sky changes when they are wives."

Astringent, worldly-wise words that bring her—where?

". . . that thou didst know how many fathom deep I am in love! But it cannot be sounded. My affection hath an unknown bottom, like the Bay of Portugal."

Another facet of this portrait is Viola whose unrequited passion for Orsino gave me sweet comfort. I was always sick of an unrequited love in those days.

> She never told her love,
> But let concealment, like a worm i' th' bud,
> Feed on her damask cheek. She pin'd in thought;
> And, with a green and yellow melancholy,
> She sat like Patience on a monument,
> Smiling at grief. Was not this love indeed?

Perhaps Juliet is the most ardent, as she awaits her lover:

> Come, gentle night; come, loving, black-brow'd night;
> Give me my Romeo; and, when I shall die,
> Take him and cut him out in little stars,
> And he will make the face of heaven so fine
> That all the world will be in love with night
> And pay no worship to the garish sun.
> O, I have bought the mansion of a love,
> But not possess'd it; and though I am sold,
> Not yet enjoy'd. So tedious is this day
> As is the night before some festival
> To an impatient child that hath new robes
> And may not wear them.

Juliet, in all her passion, never stopped to realize that such an explosive love could devastate a life, but, even if she had known, I'm sure she would have been wise enough to consider that it is better to break your heart than never to use it at all.

Portia has been my ideal of womanly dignity and graciousness, in the unquestioning way she accepts her love.

You see me, Lord Bassanio, where I stand,
Such as I am. Though for myself alone
I would not be ambitious in my wish
To wish myself much better, yet for you
I would be trebled twenty times myself,
A thousand times more fair, ten thousand times more
  rich,
That, only to stand high in your account,
I might in virtues, beauties, livings, friends,
Exceed account. But the full sum of me
Is sum of nothing, which, to term in gross,
Is an unlesson'd girl, unschool'd, unpractis'd;
Happy in this, she is not yet so old
But she may learn; happier than this,
She is not bred so dull but she can learn;
Happiest of all is that her gentle spirit
Commits itself to yours to be directed,
As from her lord, her governor, her king.
Myself and what is mine to you and yours
Is now converted. But now I was the lord
Of this fair mansion, master of my servants,
Queen o'er myself; and even now, but now,
This house, these servants, and this same myself
Are yours, my lord's. I give them with this ring; . . .

My heroine could not be too perfect, too noble—or I should have felt uncomfortable with her. So I put in a dash of Emilia. Emilia may seem a bit tart—but she makes a great deal of sense. Anyway, life with Iago must have toughened her thinking.

But I do think it is their husbands' faults
If wives do fall. Say that they slack their duties
And pour our treasures into foreign laps;
Or else break out in peevish jealousies,

Throwing restraint upon us; or say they strike us,
Or scant our former having in despite—
Why, we have galls; and though we have some grace,
Yet have we some revenge. Let husbands know
Their wives have sense like them. They see, and smell,
And have their palates both for sweet and sour,
As husbands have. What is it that they do
When they change us for others? Is it sport?
I think it is. And doth affection breed it?
I think it doth. Is't frailty that thus errs?
It is so too. And have not we affections,
Desires for sport, and frailty, as men have?
Then let them use us well; else let them know,
The ills we do, their ills instruct us so.

To make the biography of my ideal woman honest and true to life, there had to be pain as well as romance.

Constance, a mother, grieves over the death of her son:

I am not mad: this hair I tear is mine;
My name is Constance; I was Geffrey's wife;
Young Arthur is my son, and he is lost.
I am not mad. I would to heaven I were!
For then 'tis like I should forget myself.
O, if I could, what grief should I forget!
Preach some philosophy to make me mad,
For, being not mad, but sensible of grief,
My reasonable part produces reason
How I may be deliver'd of these woes,
And teaches me to kill or hang myself.
If I were mad I should forget my son,
Or madly think a babe of clouts were he:
Grief fills the room up of my absent child;
Lies in his bed, walks up and down with me,
Puts on his pretty looks, repeats his words,
Remembers me of all his gracious parts,

Stuffs out his vacant garments with his form.
O Lord! my boy, my Arthur, my fair son!
My life, my joy, my food, my all the world!

Shakespeare's women know how to love. And love, I think,
is all too rare a gift. The ultimate speech of love is Cleo-
patra's. Here she refuses to inhabit a world that doesn't
contain an Antony. When he dies, she says:

O, wither'd is the garland of the war,
The soldier's pole is fall'n! Young boys and girls
Are level now with men. The odds is gone,
And there is nothing left remarkable
Beneath the visiting moon.
My resolution's plac'd, and I have nothing
Of woman in me. Now from head to foot
I am marble-constant. Now the fleeting moon
No planet is of mine.
Hast thou the pretty worm of Nilus there
That kills and pains not? What poor an instrument
May do a noble deed! He brings me liberty.
Give me my robe, put on my crown. I have
Immortal longings in me. Now no more
The juice of Egypt's grape shall moist this lip.
Yare, yare, good Iras; quick. Methinks I hear
Antony call. I see him rouse himself
To praise my noble act. I hear him mock
The luck of Caesar, which the gods give men
To excuse their after wrath. Husband, I come!
Now to that name my courage prove my title!
I am fire and air; my other elements
I give to baser life.
Poor venomous fool,
Be angry and dispatch. O, couldst thou speak,
That I might hear thee call great Caesar ass unpoliced!
Peace, peace!

Dost thou not see my baby at my breast,
That sucks the nurse asleep?
As sweet as balm, as soft as air, as gentle—
O Antony!

And finally there's Kate—cursed Kate, sweet Kate—whose advice to wives is for all women for all time:

Thy husband is thy lord, thy life, thy keeper,
Thy head, thy sovereign; one that cares for thee,
And for thy maintenance; commits his body
To painful labour both by sea and land,
To watch the night in storms, the day in cold,
Whilst thou li'st warm at home, secure and safe;
And craves no other tribute at thy hands
But love, fair looks, and true obedience—
Too little payment for so great a debt.
Such duty as the subject owes the prince,
Even such a woman oweth to her husband;
And when she is froward, peevish, sullen, sour,
And not obedient to his honest will,
What is she but a foul contending rebel
And graceless traitor to her loving lord?
I am asham'd that women are so simple
To offer war where they should kneel for peace;
Or seek for rule, supremacy, and sway
When they are bound to serve, love, and obey.
Why are our bodies soft and weak and smooth,
Unapt to toil and trouble in the world,
But that our soft conditions and our hearts
Should well agree with our external parts?
Come, come, you froward and unable worms!
My mind hath been as big as one of yours,
My heart as great, my reason haply more,
To bandy word for word and frown for frown;
But now I see our lances are but straws,

Our strength as weak, our weakness past compare,
That seeming to be most which we indeed least are.
Then vail your stomachs, for it is no boot,
And place your hands below your husband's foot:
In token of which duty, if he please,
My hand is ready; may it do him ease.

There you have my heroine—the companion of my youth, the comfort of all my years.

Although my portrait is finished, may my heroine have one last speech about love? It is a man's speech, that of Berowne in *Love's Labour's Lost*, but I believe it could have been spoken by a woman.

A lover's eyes will gaze an eagle blind.
A lover's ear will hear the lowest sound
When the suspicious head of theft is stopp'd.
Love's feeling is more soft and sensible
Than are the tender horns of cockled snails.
Love's tongue proves dainty Bacchus gross in taste.
For valour, is not Love a Hercules,
Still climbing trees in the Hesperides?
Subtle as Sphinx; as sweet and musical
As bright Apollo's lute, strung with his hair.
And when Love speaks, the voice of all the gods
Make heaven drowsy with the harmony.
Never durst poet touch a pen to write
Until his ink were temp'red with Love's sighs;
O, then his lines would ravish savage ears
And plant in tyrants mild humility.
From women's eyes this doctrine I derive.
They sparkle still the right Promethean fire;
They are the books, the arts, the academes,
That show, contain, and nourish all the world.
Else none at all in aught proves excellent.

Favorite Performances

PEOPLE, a curious inquisitive breed, are forever asking actors which role he or she enjoyed playing the most. It is one of a multitude of familiar maddening questions every actor faces repeatedly throughout his lifetime, from the young and the old, wherever he is, at dinner parties, backstage, during interviews, or on vacation. "Are you nervous on opening night?" "What is the secret of great acting?" "Should I go into the theater?" "How do you develop talent?" And finally, "Which is your favorite role?" That last question is as fazing as the one foolishly put to a mother—"Which of your children have you loved the best?"

There are various reasons for an actor accepting a role, and these, of course, include both his need to feed himself and his need to practice his art. But, pragmatic considerations aside, not the least of the reasons usually is that he has fallen in love with the character he has been asked to play. I have always—well, nearly always—agreed to appear in a play because the character I would portray—for some subtle, intangible, elusive, and undefinable reason—caught my imagination and my affection. Each had its own distinctive appeal so that even now as I look back over three-score years on the stage I cannot in my heart choose favorites. Nor, I suppose, would I want to.

But I can make a confession. I treasure above all others my recollections of three single performances; performances that have given me the greatest gratification in my career. Perhaps they have their special appeal because I did them for me, for me only—not for a paying audience in a regular theater, and because in them I was uninhibited, and free. If you will excuse the expression, I was able to "ham" them up; and I gloried in the chance. In fact, at the time, after each of these performances, I gave myself a great accolade. I did something that I have never allowed myself to do in the theater. I burst into tears. That sort of self-indulgence was knocked out of me when I was very young, when I was taught that self-discipline was practically the most important thing in acting on the stage, that one must never indulge oneself in that kind of emotional orgy (or in too much enjoyment of what one is doing, either). This, I was taught, was embarrassing to an audience. Fanny Brice used to say, "If you cry, they don't."

Sometimes I wish I could break this habit, this self-discipline, and allow myself the kind of blessed indulgence and emotional license that I occasionally see in the young actors of today and which is very impressive to everyone in the audience, including me. But always there is that basic training to rise up and remind me that in my acting I must try to hold a little part of me aloof, objective, so that I can, so to speak, stand aside and edit what I am doing. This is what was drummed into me in my youth and through the years. There can be no change—on stage, that is. It seems that off

stage I do once in a while cut loose, though I think of myself as a most unactressy sort of person. At least that's what
people tell me. Ruth Gordon, for instance, declared that
during a small tornado in Nyack I ran to the window, flung
out my arms, threw back my head, and cried above the
uproar, "Hold fast, my trees!" I could swear I never did—
but then, I was pretty excited at the time.

Again, Eduardo Rendon, a Mexican friend, says he first
believed I was a real actress the time I tried to describe to
him a newborn volcano, Parícutin, which I had gone on
horseback to view way down in Uruapan in southwestern
Mexico. I struggled along with words for a while, he reports,
then finally gave up, and acted the whole thing out. There,
in the MacArthurs' moon-drenched garden, with bougainvillea for a backdrop, he says I gave an inspired interpreta-
tion of a volcano.

It's nice to hear about those forgotten bursts of histrionics,
but I never shall need to be reminded of my three favorite
performances. How I reveled in them! With no audience
to be responsible to, there was no need to edit and I could
enjoy myself. I did, with all the stops out.

The first of these performances took place shortly after
the war. I was appearing in London in *The Glass Menagerie*.
During one of my social engagements I expressed a desire
to visit Middle Temple Hall, which was reported to be then
in the final stages of its reconstruction following the devas-
tating Nazi bombings in 1940. The hall was part of the
Middle Temple, one of the four historic Inns of Court, begun
during the reign of Edward I. These Inns were societies or
colleges accommodating benchers, barristers, and law students (the benchers being senior members who ran the
societies). In addition to having quarters there, the students
learned law and divinity, as well as music and dancing. It

was their custom to devise plays, masques, and assorted revels for their own entertainment and the entertainment of their guests. Most celebrated for these frolics were the Gray's Inn and the Middle Temple.

I was especially interested in Middle Temple Hall because it was there that Shakespeare's own company, the Chamberlain's Men, had given one of the earliest performances of *Twelfth Night* in connection with Candlemas festivities in February 1602. It had been this same troupe, by the way, that had performed the play in 1600 for Queen Elizabeth and her guests at the annual Twelfth Night Revels. When word came of the destruction of Middle Temple Hall, I happened to be playing Viola in *Twelfth Night* to Maurice Evans' Malvolio. I cannot describe the anguish and heartache we all felt then. But I also remember how I was struck once again with the durability and the strength of words. I remember thinking with some emotion how wrong Shakespeare had proved himself to be. In one of his sonnets he utters these lines:

> Since brass, nor stone, nor earth, nor boundless sea
> But sad mortality o'ersways their power,
> How with this rage shall beauty hold a plea,
> Whose action is no stronger than a flower?

Poor man, to have had these doubts. Four hundred years later, though the theater in which *Twelfth Night* had once played to joy and laughter lay shattered by rage, this same play, its beauty as fresh as ever, was flourishing in a theater in New York City.

A friend of mine, a member of Parliament, made the arrangements for me to see the restoration of Middle Temple Hall. He had an apartment in the Temple, and one afternoon we had tea there with his aunt. Then we went over to the hall. As he showed me around, he related how the bombs actually had leveled the old building to the ground. Not a stone was left on stone. But curiously enough, that stage where once the original creators of Orsino, Olivia, and Viola had acted, had remained intact when the debris was cleared away after the fires died down. We went below to see why. That stage had been made of the trunks of oak trees—the whole length of the trunk having been split down the middle and the two sections placed side by side. Underneath one could see the round sides of the trunks. Those trunks provided tremendous strength, and not even the bombs could shake that stage.

We returned to the main floor. The workmen on the scaffolding were putting the finishing touches to their labor and I was filled with a kind of exaltation. In my mind's eye I had a vision of Will standing in this hall centuries before, when it was new, wondering why he had chosen to be a playwright, asking himself why not an architect or a builder so that his work would have a chance to endure for the ages. I could see him standing against a column there by the stage, watching the performance of *Twelfth Night,* his gentle, little play, almost the prettiest, the most lyrical of all, and thinking, "My poor little play, my poor little words. They are gone as soon as they come out of the actors' mouths. How ephemeral they are compared to the solidity of this beautiful stone building." I admit that my fancy had run amok. I wanted to leap back across the centuries to comfort him, to say, "It's all right, old man. Your play is still going strong." I could no longer restrain myself. I left my friend, jumped onto the stage and, though it was several years now since my last performance in *Twelfth Night,* I began reciting Viola's great speech to Olivia, a denier of love.

If I did love you in my master's flame
With such a suff'ring, such a deadly life,
In your denial I would find no sense;
I would not understand it.

(*Olivia.* Why, what would you?)

Make me a willow cabin at your gate
And call upon my soul within the house;
Write loyal cantons of contemned love
And sing them loud even in the dead of night;
Halloa your name to the reverberate hills
And make the babbling gossip of the air
Cry out 'Olivia!' O, you should not rest
Between the elements of air and earth
But you should pity me!

There was a dead silence as I finished. The men on the scaffolding had halted their work. Then they applauded, as did my friend. And I cried.

Another of my favorite performances took place in Corinth, old Corinth, or what is left of it.

I had been on a motor tour of Greece, careening around that fascinating country with a young couple whom I dearly love, the Kenneth Volks. Needless to say, it had been a grand and awesome experience: the bustling, modern city of Athens; the Acropolis with its ruins—those indescribably beautiful and precious remains of the golden age of architecture; the Propylaea, the Parthenon, the Erechtheion, the Temple of the Wingless Victory; and, among the pine trees on the slopes, the Temples of Aphrodite and Eros, the Fountain of Clepsydra, the Theater of Dionysus, and the hill of the Pnyx, that place of popular assembly where Pericles and other lesser politicians and statesmen addressed the crowds much in the manner that orators hold forth to this day in Hyde Park. Of course we'd driven through Thebes and Levadia and Arakhova; we'd taken the long, breathtaking road that twists and turns its way into the mountains overlooking the greenish-hued Corinthian Gulf, leading to the sanctuary of Apollo—Delphi, where the celebrated Pythia delivered her oracles.

And so, already filled with our share of wonder, our minds and imaginations already racing with these reminders of the past, we set out from Athens to Corinth, traveling over the new coast road that frequently flanks the Saronic Gulf. And, after crossing the Corinthian Canal, we found ourselves in old Corinth. We visited the museum, the Temple of Apollo which had been built some time in the 6th century B.C., the Fountain of Peirene, and the Agora. The Agora, or marketplace, stirred me especially. For, in addition to all the other mental images that this sort of journey into time has a way of creating, I thrilled to the fact that it had been historically verified that St. Paul had worked and spoken in ancient Corinth. Indeed, it was to his congregation here that he wrote two of his most famous epistles, those two letters that probably contain the best formulation and noblest expression of his ethical values.

Perhaps there was something especially intoxicating in the climate of that sunny day. Perhaps the sun had been a little too strong. But as I walked around I seemed to have jolted myself into the ages and I was terribly moved. When we came to the Rostrum, a little marble slab from which a speaker could look downward to his listeners, our guide explained its use: "Anyone who had something he wished to say could wait his turn, climb on the platform, and harangue the populace." As an afterthought, he let drop

"St. Paul is supposed to have spoken from here. Follow me."
And he was off to the next site in a great hurry. He was a
kind of hint and run liar, that guide. Usually our trio followed behind him, suppressing giggles. But that day I didn't
move. I stood gaping at that slab of white marble willing
myself to believe that Paul of Tarsus, a man of flesh and
blood, had once stood there. The soles of his sandals had
pressed on this stone, his voice had sounded in this air. I
became possessed of a terrible, an irresistible impulse. Shaking inside, I took a quick look to see that everyone within
sight and hearing distance was dark complexioned and
looked Greek. I hoped they understood no English, because
what I was about to do might have been considered irrever-
ent coming from someone in an old sundress. Assuring myself that I would not be understood by anyone I mounted the
Rostrum and called out loud and clear, as to a bustling
crowd, the words I had to hear in that place.

> Though I speak with the tongues of men and of
> angels, and have not charity, I am become as sounding
> brass, or a tinkling cymbal.
> And though I have the gift of prophecy, and under-
> stand all mysteries, and all knowledge; and though I
> have all faith, so that I could remove mountains, and
> have not charity, I am nothing.
> And though I bestow all my goods to feed the poor,
> and though I give my body to be burned, and have not
> charity, it profiteth me nothing.
> Charity suffereth long, and is kind; charity envieth
> not; charity vaunteth not itself, is not puffed up,
> Doth not behave itself unseemly, seeketh not her
> own, is not easily provoked, thinketh no evil;
> Rejoiceth not in iniquity, but rejoiceth in truth;
> Beareth all things, believeth all things, hopeth all
> things, endureth all things.

Charity never faileth: but whether there be prophe-
cies, they shall fail; whether there be tongues, they shall
cease; whether there be knowledge, it shall vanish
away.

For we know in part, and we prophesy in part.

But when that which is perfect is come, then that
which is in part shall be done away.

When I was a child, I spake as a child, I understood
as a child, I thought as a child: but when I became a
man, I put away childish things.

For now we see through a glass, darkly; but then face
to face: now I know in part; but then shall I know even
as also I am known.

And now abideth faith, hope, charity, these three; but
the greatest of these is charity.

Corinth is the gateway to the Peloponnesus, and we set off
on the exhilarating journey to the many fabled sites we know
from our reading of plays, verse, and history: Mount
Olympus, sanctuary of Zeus; Mycenae, at the foot of Mount
Zara, with its Lion Gate, and the tombs of Agamemnon and
Clytemnestra (they had just uncovered a new tomb which
our guide, the blessed liar, assured us was Orestes');
Nauplia, first capital of modern Greece; and then over the
road to the coast and Epidaurus. All over the mainland we
had found the Grecian countryside utterly marvelous—the
plains and mountains, the waterways and lakes. The mountains are especially rugged, wild, and fascinating. Going over
the mountainous road of the Peloponnesus, it occurred to
me again, as it had many times before on our little trip, how
easy it was for all those ancient legends to have grown up,
how easy it must have been to believe them. My own imagination was now soaring once again as we passed through
Arcadia. I kept looking, slightly in eagerness and slightly in

terror, for Pan to be darting from tree to tree, keeping an eye on our car as we went along. I think I really believed it for a while and I remember getting a little nervous lest I be going out of my head.

Epidaurus turned out to be the highlight of our wanderings, the setting for perhaps my favorite performance. Here stands the sanctuary of Asclepius, known throughout Greece for his healing powers. Here the sacred grove was filled over the years with offerings of those who had been cured of their afflictions. And here came not only those in quest of help from the god but also those who wanted to participate in or watch the athletic and dramatic festivals that occurred every four years in his honor. One can still see the ruins of the Gymnasium, the Palestra, the Tholos, the Stoa, the Xenon, and the temples.

But the miracle of Epidaurus, the miracle that I was most anxious to see, was its theater. Built in the 4th century B.C. by the Argive architect, Polycleitus the Younger, it is the last pure Greek theater of classic times, unchanged by the Romans who went around changing theaters and their shape. The theater at Epidaurus is the kind of pure Greek theater that was in use when Aeschylus wrote the first play.

Set in this holy precinct of Epidaurus, enclosed by the surrounding hills and ravines, this theater revives in the imagination something of the ancient atmosphere of the days when the old festivals took place. Your first impression as you enter is that of size. To us in this twentieth century it is always startling as we travel through the ancient world to realize that those people thousands of years ago had anything so large. The theater at Epidaurus rises, stone row on stone row, against the hills, and when filled can seat 14,500 spectators. And to embellish this miracle, the acoustics are superb. Even a whisper from the oval stage at the base of those tiers can be heard in the uppermost row. To prove the point, tourist guides always put on what I think is a somewhat ridiculous performance, a desecration in this theater with its memories of magnificence. They take their place in the center of the stage, having sent the tourists to the last row, and strike a match. Everyone, of course, oohs and ahs because he has heard the match strike. The guides drop a penny on the turf stage, the sound is heard, and the same reaction occurs again. By the grace of God the theater was empty when we arrived there and I did not have to participate in such antics. I had my own way of testing acoustics. We had brought some Greek plays with us to Athens so that we could read them when we went to the theater. Among them was Euripides' *The Trojan Women* which contains one of my most beloved passages in all of the stage's literature, Hecuba's lament over her dead grandson.

I don't think there has ever been a better speech written for an actress. The lines are vivid, human—an extraordinary articulation of what every older person feels when he or she has to bury a young person. Those lines have a special significance for me, and when I need them they bring me comfort—comfort in the knowledge that even back there, thousands of years ago, people knew and understood the same tragic struggle. Hecuba's lines beginning with "Oh man, secure when once good fortune comes" and ending with "No one is ever always fortunate" are, to me, the distillation of sublime wisdom.

I took my little play out there with me onto the stage of this absolutely empty theater and, like one of those tyrannical guides, sent my two young friends climbing up to the very last row. Then, in a soft voice, hardly above a whisper, certainly no louder than a conversational voice, I read Hecuba's lament. And it was so nice to read it in that voice because I didn't have to depend on any of the artificial projection demanded by our own theaters. And I knew, as I read the passage, that I was playing Hecuba on a stage where some other actress must have played the role all those centuries ago when it was fresh, and I knew too that I would probably never have another chance to play it on another stage—anywhere. I do not have the size for it; and, even if someone asked me to do it, I would refuse. But there in Epidaurus I could really let go, honestly let go and indulge myself. And toward the end of the speech I became so moved both by the lines and the intoxicating pleasure of the moment that I could barely get the words out even in a small whisper.

Set the shield down—the great round shield of Hector.
I wish I need not look at it.
You Greeks, your spears are sharp but not your wits.
You feared a child. You murdered him.
Strange murder. You were frightened, then? You
    thought
he might build up our ruined Troy? And yet
when Hector fought and thousands at his side,
we fell beneath you. Now, when all is lost,
the city captured and the Trojans dead,
a little child like this made you afraid.
The fear that comes when reason goes away—
Myself, I do not wish to share it.
Beloved, what a death has come to you.
If you had fallen fighting for the city,
If you had known strong youth and love
and godlike power, if we could think
you had known happiness—if there is
happiness anywhere—
But now—you saw and knew, but with your soul

you did not know, and what was in your house
you could not use.
Poor little one. How savagely our ancient walls,
Apollo's towers, have torn away the curls
your mother's fingers wound and where she pressed
her kisses—here where the broken bone grins white—
Oh no—I cannot—
Dear hands, the same dear shape your father's had,
how loosely now you fall. And dear proud lips
forever closed. False words you spoke to me
when you would jump into my bed, call me sweet
    names
and tell me, Grandmother, when you are dead,
I'll cut off a great lock of hair and lead my soldiers all
to ride out past your tomb.
Not you, but I, old, homeless, childless,
must lay you in your grave, so young,
so miserably dead.
Dear God. How you would run to greet me.
And I would nurse you in my arms, and oh,
so sweet to watch you sleep. All gone.
What could a poet carve upon your tomb?
"A child lies here whom the Greeks feared and slew."
Ah, Greece should boast of that.
Child, they have taken all that was your father's,
but one thing, for your burying, you shall have,
the bronze-barred shield.
It kept safe Hector's mighty arm, but now
it has lost its master.
The grip of his own hand has marked it—dear to me
    then—
His sweat has stained the rim. Often and often
in battle it rolled down from brows and beard
while Hector held the shield close.
Come, bring such covering for the pitiful dead body
as we still have. God has not left us much

to make a show with. Everything I have
I give you, child.
    O men, secure when once good fortune comes—
fools, fools. Fortune's ways—
here now, there now. She springs
away—back—and away, an idiot's dance.
No one is ever always fortunate.

    My eyes were welling up, but I held back my tears. Then
my friends rejoined me, telling me how wonderful it all had
been, how they had heard every syllable, even at the end.

Rooms

Not so long ago a friend brought me a short poem by the Chinese poet Feng Chih. It is called "The Room and the Windows," and this is the way it goes:

Often we spent an intimate night
In a strange room, and we did not know
How it looked during the day,
And we knew less of its past and its future.
We saw the infinite landscape beyond the window.
And we remembered the dim road
Through which we had come at dusk. That was all we
    knew.
Departing tomorrow, we shall never return.
Close your eyes! Let those intimate nights
And unfamiliar places be woven into our hearts.
Our life is a landscape beyond the windows,
And there in the descending light we discern

A tree, the glimmer of lake water, infinite visions
Which rise from the forgotten past and the fading
  future.

Anyone who has spent a great part of his life in travel will
read those lines with a slight pang. I did, because immediately and with a burst of memory that hurt a little, I
thought of all the rooms Charlie and I had occupied and
had gone away from. Especially that one in Limoges,
France.

Charlie and I had been on a wine-tasting trip through the
Burgandy country on the way to Carcassonne, and we had
stopped at Limoges to spend the night. The hotel we went
to was an old-fashioned one. We were shown to our room
and Charlie took one look around, saw the great big red
roses on the wallpaper and the great big very fancy brass
bed and the washstand with the pitcher and the bowl and
the *pot de chambre* and said, "Well, Helen, you may never
have been in one, I hope, but I think you are about to spend
the night in a French bordello."

When I think of all the hotel rooms in which I have lived
from the time my mother and I left Washington in search of
my career, I realize that there were hundreds—of which I
couldn't possibly describe or remember more than a few.
They have ranged everywhere from rooms over bars to
awesome presidential suites.

When we first came to New York, we had a room in Mrs.
Nathanson's theatrical boarding house on Lexington Avenue.
Now, there was a dreary one—a back room with a double
bed that took up the whole darn place and you had to kind
of squinch around it.

Then, with a special fondness, I remember the rooms that

we shared with the Hess Sisters when we were on tour with a musical called *Summer Widowers*. We shared because that was much cheaper—two rooms and a bath between us. And what I liked was going out with the Hess Sisters and my mother after the show to one of those all-night snack places and having a wonderful sandwich supper—always a delight to my soul. In the morning I would go into the next room where the sisters would be practicing their Russian dance steps, and I would practice with them.

Later, on another tour, we shared a room with a darling girl, Pat Leeds. She was the girlfriend of the leading comedian in the show, Hugh Monroe, and they lived together. But when the company manager reported back to Lew Fields in New York that there was a lot of this sort of doubling up going on in the company, Mr. Fields sent back word that it had to stop. So Pat joined up with mother and me and we had a most delightful time. She was full of stories of the English theater and the Christmas pantomime in which she had once played the robin who covered the poor little babes-in-the-woods with leaves. (As the run progressed she became known to the company as the "damn robin.") And I might say that none of us ever gave any thought to Miss Leeds and her boyfriend. In the theater I've met all kinds of women—call them shady characters, ladies of easy virtue, or anything else—but I've never met people who were more careful and considerate or more militant about protecting the morals of a child than they were. Many of the women I've known since have shocked me a lot more than girls like Pat Leeds.

I was fourteen when I appeared with John Drew in *The Prodigal Husband* and went off on my first tour of one-night stands. Drew, of course, was one of the theater's great matinee idols. He was everyone's idea of a gentleman, the man of eternal good manners, faultless breeding, unvarying grace. He was the epitome of nonchalance and savoir-faire.

Lionel Barrymore, whose uncle he was, once said, "Uncle Jack deserves the highest honors of all the members of our family, for it is so much harder to be a great gentleman than a great actor."

Well, John Drew always wanted the ladies of his company to ride in parlor cars. You just couldn't ride in the coach, even though you had to pay the extra fare yourself—and none of us were earning very much money in those days. He insisted that he wanted the members of his company to be ladies and gentlemen, to uphold the dignity of the theater. I accepted it then without question. Now I understand it better. He wanted the theater to look good to the world; he didn't want actors to be the rogues and vagabonds they had traditionally been thought to be. And he insisted that we live in the best hotels. But once in a while my poor mother, who was trying to cut a corner here or there—we were both living on my small salary—would get us off to a boarding-house when she heard of a good one. I must say I liked those boardinghouses. They generally were snug and gave me the feeling that I was in a home. But when Drew found this out one time in Philadelphia, he was shocked. And he sent John Henry Mears, the company manager, to check on the respectability of the place mother had chosen.

As my career grew and changed, so did my rooms. Although I would have sworn to anybody that I was the most normal, cut-and-dried, unstylish kind of person, I did indulge myself. As early as *Coquette*, in which I toured shortly after my marriage, I began to need more space. For one thing, because I felt I needed more exercise than the daily walks I had been taking, I began carting a ping-pong table around with me. And that could be accommodated only in one of those hotel sample rooms, the ones that salesmen use when they go to a town to show their wares. Members of my companies would come and spell each other, as they did on my walks, playing ping-pong into the night. I also got to carrying my own sheets and pillowcases, some silk ones that Charlie had given me for trains so that I didn't have to sleep on the bad linens they provided. Add to these my down pillows, blue moiré down comforter, and countless knickknacks that gave me the security of familiar things, plus a radio and phonograph to beguile me. In addition—I think it was about the time of *Victoria Regina* that I became very conscious of art—I carried a whole set of Toulouse-Lautrec prints, and wherever I went those awful French engravings with the fancy frames would come off the walls of the hotel rooms and my Lautrecs would go up. It was like the procession of a royal duke or something.

One of the rooms I remember vividly was the one I had during the *Mary of Scotland* tour. We had our own special train for that tour, and I had a drawingroom that was my home for about three or four nights out of every week. During each week we'd play about two nights in one place— Friday and Saturday in the larger cities—and the other nights were one-night stands. We would go into a town, give the performance, go back to the train after the performance and take off for the next town, like in the circus. I felt as though I were something of a housewife in my little drawingroom. I had the walls all decorated and it was like having a little home. I was very happy. It was a nice feeling to get in there and go off to the next place and know nobody was going to phone me or say could you please see my daughter who wants to be an actress.

Well, I don't lug a ping-pong table any more, or those Lautrecs. And I don't take my own sheets and pillowcases

either. I don't do anything that foolish now. I sleep on whatever linen there is, and I don't notice the difference. In those
other days it just seemed normal and pretty average for me
to feel I needed all those fancy things. But now, when I look
back, I think I prefer the plainest room I've ever been in to
any of the sumptuous suites.

I eventually learned that there is no loneliness so acute for
me as that which I feel when I'm touring and somebody is
trying to pretend for me that I am really at home. More
recently, when I have gone on tour I have usually told the
company manager that I want one room, please, a nice room
with sun coming through the windows; none of those big
awesome suites. I have a big, pretty room at home that I
love, and those enormous hotel suites only remind me of it
by pretending to be substitutes.

Yet you'd be surprised how hard it is for me to get that
simple little room with the sun streaming through the windows. The company manager and the hotel manager seem to
think that I'm pennypinching and more often than not they
stick me into a skating rink of a place and charge me the
price of a regular room. And there I am knowing the full
feeling of loneliness, because there will be the kitchenette,
there will be the refrigerator, there will be all the glasses and
the dishes and two or three bedrooms and that enormous
living room with all the trimmings and usually the perma-
nent odor of cigarettes in the upholstery and everything else
that indicates the parties that have taken place there before.
The rooms call for people and laughter and conversation and
drinks, and I'm in them all by myself. I think nobody loves
me and I haven't a friend in the world, and I begin thinking
of what a dreary and isolated and sad life I lead. I really get
very depressed in those places. So my custom is to get the
key to the bedroom and go in there and never ever look into

that great big awful elaborate thing that I've been given by
the conscientious and solicitous management of the hotel.
The smaller hotel rooms of America from away back have
been pretty characterless, and that I like. I'm for that. I
didn't used to be. But I am now.

From BUDDENBROOKS

They were sitting in the "landscape-room" on the first
floor of the rambling old house in Meng Street, which
the firm of Johann Buddenbrook had acquired some time
since, though the family had not lived in it long. The
room was hung with heavy resilient tapestries put up in
such a way that they stood well out from the walls.
They were woven in soft tones to harmonize with the
carpet, and they depicted idyllic landscapes in the style
of the eighteenth century, with merry vine-dressers,
busy husbandmen, and gaily beribboned shepherdesses
who sat beside crystal streams with spotless lambs in
their laps or exchanged kisses with amorous shepherds.
These scenes were usually lighted by a pale yellow sunset to match the yellow coverings on the white enam-
elled furniture and the yellow silk curtains at the two
windows.

For the size of the room, the furniture was rather
scant. A round table, its slender legs decorated with fine
lines of gilding, stood, not in front of the sofa, but by the
wall opposite the little harmonium, on which lay a flute-
case; some stiff arm-chairs were ranged in a row round
the walls; there was a sewing-table by the window, and
a flimsy ornamental writing-desk laden with knickknacks.

On the other side of the room from the windows was
a glass door, through which one looked into the semi-
darkness of a pillared hall; and on the left were the lofty

white folding doors that led to the dining-room. A semi-circular niche in the remaining wall was occupied by the stove, which crackled away behind a polished wrought-iron screen.

THOMAS MANN

From WUTHERING HEIGHTS

One step brought us into the family sitting-room, without any introductory lobby or passage: they call it here "the house" pre-eminently. It includes kitchen and parlour, generally; but I believe at Wuthering Heights the kitchen is forced to retreat altogether into another quarter: at least I distinguished a chatter of tongues, and a clatter of culinary utensils, deep within; and I observed no signs of roasting, boiling, or baking, about the huge fire-place; nor any glitter of copper saucepans and tin cullenders on the walls. One end, indeed, reflected splendidly both light and heat from ranks of immense pewter dishes, interspersed with silver jugs and tankards, towering row after row, on a vast oak dresser, to the very roof. The latter had never been underdrawn: its entire anatomy lay bare to an inquiring eye, except where a frame of wood laden with oatcakes and clusters of legs of beef, mutton, and ham, concealed it. Above the chimney were sundry villainous old guns, and a couple of horse-pistols: and, by way of ornament, three gaudily-painted canisters disposed along its ledge. The floor was of smooth white stone; the chairs, high-backed, primitive structures, painted green: one or two heavy black ones lurking in the shade. In an arch under the dresser, reposed a huge, liver-coloured bitch pointer, surrounded by a swarm of squealing puppies; and other dogs haunted other recesses.

EMILY BRONTË

From SWANN'S WAY

These shifting and confused gusts of memory never lasted for more than a few seconds; it often happened that, in my spell of uncertainty as to where I was, I did not distinguish the successive theories of which that uncertainty was composed any more than when we watch a horse running, we isolate the successive positions of its body as they appear upon a bioscope. But I had seen first one and then another of the rooms in which I had slept during my life, and in the end I would revisit them all in the long course of my waking dream: rooms in winter, where on going to bed I would at once bury my head in a nest, built up out of the most diverse materials, the corner of my pillow, the top of my blankets, a piece of a shawl, the edge of my bed, and a copy of an evening paper, all of which things I would contrive, with the infinite patience of birds building their nests, to cement into one whole; rooms where, in a keen frost, I would feel the satisfaction of being shut in from the outer world (like the sea-swallow which builds at the end of a dark tunnel and is kept warm by the surrounding earth), and where, the fire keeping in all night, I would sleep wrapped up, as it were, in a great cloak of snug and savoury air, shot with the glow of the logs which would break out again in flame: in a sort of alcove without walls, a cave of warmth dug out of the heart of the room itself, a zone of heat whose boundaries were constantly shifting and altering in temperature as gusts of air ran across them to strike freshly upon my face, from the corners of the room, or from parts near the window or far from the fireplace which had therefore remained cold—or rooms in summer, where I would delight to feel myself a part of the warm evening, where the moonlight striking upon the half-opened shutters would throw down to the foot of my bed its enchanted ladder; where I would fall asleep, as it might be in the open air, like a titmouse which the breeze keeps poised in the focus of a sunbeam—or sometimes the Louis XVI room, so cheerful that I could never feel really unhappy, even on my first night in it: that room where the slender columns which lightly supported its ceiling would part, ever so gracefully, to indicate where the bed was and to keep it separate; sometimes again that little room with the high ceiling, hollowed in the form of a pyramid out of two separate storeys, and partly walled with mahogany, in which from the first moment my mind was drugged by the unfamiliar scent of flowering grasses, convinced of the hostility of the violet curtains and of the insolent indifference of a clock that chattered on at the top of its voice as though I were not there; while a strange and pitiless mirror with square feet, which stood across one corner of the room, cleared for itself a site I had not looked to find tenanted in the quiet surroundings of my normal field of vision: that room in which my mind, forcing itself for hours on end to leave its moorings, to elongate itself upwards so as to take on the exact shape of the room, and to reach to the summit of that monstrous funnel, had passed so many anxious nights while my body lay stretched out in bed, my eyes staring upwards, my ears straining, my nostrils sniffing uneasily, and my heart beating; until custom had changed the colour of the curtains, made the clock keep quiet, brought an expression of pity to the cruel, slanting face of the glass, disguised or even completely dispelled the scent of flowering grasses, and distinctly reduced the apparent loftiness of the ceiling. Custom! that skilful but unhurrying manager who begins by torturing the mind for weeks on end with her provisional arrangements; whom the mind, for all that, is fortunate in discovering, for without the help of custom it would never contrive, by its own efforts, to make any room seem habitable.

Among the rooms which used most commonly to take shape in my mind during my long nights of sleeplessness, there was none that differed more utterly from the rooms at Combray, thickly powdered with the motes of an atmosphere granular, pollenous, edible and instinct with piety, than my room in the Grand Hôtel de la Plage, at Balbec, the walls of which, washed with ripolin, contained, like the polished sides of a basin in which the water glows with a blue, lurking fire, a finer air, pure, azure-tinted, saline. The Bavarian upholsterer who had been entrusted with the furnishing of this hotel had varied his scheme of decoration in different rooms, and in that which I found myself occupying had set against the walls, on three sides of it, a series of low book-cases with glass fronts, in which, according to where they stood, by a law of nature which he had, perhaps, forgotten to take into account, was reflected this or that section of the ever-changing view of the sea, so that the walls were lined with a frieze of sea-scapes, interrupted only by the polished mahogany of the actual shelves. And so effective was this that the whole room had the appearance of one of those model bedrooms which you see nowadays in Housing Exhibitions, decorated with works of art which are calculated by their designer to refresh the eyes of whoever may ultimately have to sleep in the rooms, the subjects being kept in some degree of harmony with the locality and surroundings of the houses for which the rooms are planned.

MARCEL PROUST

From PÈRE GORIOT

Intended by nature to serve as a boarding-house, the Maison Vauquer has on the ground floor a front room which may be entered by a French window, and which has, besides, two other windows facing the street. It adjoins the dining room, which is separated from the kitchen by the staircase, the steps of which are of checkered wood and waxed. Nothing could be more somber than the front room, the salon, where the furniture is covered with horsehair in stripes alternately dull and glossy. In the middle there is a round marble-topped table, with, for ornament, a tea service in white porcelain with half-faded gold bands, of the sort that is to be seen everywhere today. The floor is far from even; the wainscotting rises to elbow-height; and the rest of the wall is hung with a varnished paper representing the principal scenes from *Télémaque,* with the classic personages in color. The panel between the two barred windows exhibits to the guests the feast offered by Calypso to Ulysses' son. For forty years this picture has stimulated the humor of the young boarders who try to forget their poor estate by making fun of the dinners to which it condemns them. The stone mantel, with a fireplace so clean that obviously it is used only on notable occasions, has for ornaments two vases with faded artificial flowers under glass and a blue marble clock in the most atrocious taste.

There is an odor in this room for which the language has no name, and which we must call a boarding-house smell. It is close, mildewed and rancid: it makes one shiver with cold, it makes the nose damp, it penetrates one's clothes; it smells like a room in which dinner has just been eaten: it stinks of the kitchen, the scullery, the hospital. Perhaps it could be described if someone had

found the terms for cataloguing the nauseating elements
that come forth from the unique catarrhal breaths of
all the boarders, young and old.

Well! Despite its being so horrible, if you were to
compare this room with the dining room which is next
to it, you would think that the drawing room was as
elegant and sweet-smelling as a boudoir should be. The
dining room, where the walls are paneled to the ceiling,
was long ago painted in some color which cannot be
discerned today, and is now only a background on which
layers of dirt have formed in such a fashion as to present some bizarre designs. The room is surrounded by
sticky buffets holding carafes which are dirty and
chipped, round mats with a metallic sheen, piles of
plates of thick blue-bordered porcelain, manufactured
at Tournai. In a corner there is a box with numbered
pigeonholes for the stained and spotted napkins of the
boarders. The room has those indestructible pieces of
furniture, proscribed from every other place, and resting there just as the refuse of humanity come to rest in
homes for the incurable. You would see there a barom-
eter with a monk who comes forth when it points to
rain, engravings so horrible as to spoil one's appetite
and all framed in varnished black wood with gold stripes,
a tortoise-shell clock case inlaid with copper, a green
stove, Argand lamps, in which dust mixes with oil, and
a long table covered with oil cloth so greasy that a merry
boarder can write his name on it with the end of his
finger. And there are rickety chairs, and little piteous
hempen mats which slip away under one's feet but
never vanish for good, and broken footwarmers with
hinges that no longer work and with their wooden parts
burnt away. To explain how old this furniture is, how
cracked and rotten and shaky and worn, how deformed,
how lopsided, and sick and dying, we should have to
embark on a description which would too long delay

our start on the story and which hurried readers would not pardon. The red tiles of the floor are full of indentations caused by waxing and painting. In short, this is the kingdom of poverty without poetry: a poverty which is economical, concentrated, threadbare. If it is not yet filthy, it is spotted; if it has not holes and rags, it is about to rot away.

HONORÉ DE BALZAC

My favorite room in a play is the stage set for S. N. Behrman's *Biography*. Behrman says of this room that it has the mellowness of anachronism. I think several of the rooms in my Nyack home have this quality. These are not cluttered rooms; but they do have echoes of the past. And everyone who comes into them finds these echoes warm and mellow. Professional decorators have more than once tried talking me into re-doing them. And the one time I was really tempted it was my son who stopped me in the nick of time. Here, then, is the room that is the setting of *Biography*.

SCENE: The studio-apartment of Marion Froude in an old fashioned studio building in West 57th St., New York. A great, cavernous room expressing in its polyglot furnishings the artistic patois of the various landlords who have sublet this apartment to wandering tenants like Marion Froude. The styles range from medieval Florence to contemporary Grand Rapids; on a movable raised platform in the center is a papal throne chair in red velvet and gold fringes. Not far from it is an ordinary American kitchen chair. The hanging lamp which sheds a mellow light over a French Empire sofa is filigreed copper Byzantine. Another and longer sofa across the room against the grand piano is in soft green velvet and has the gentility of a polite Park Avenue drawing room. Under the stairs, rear, which go up to Marion's bedroom, are stacks of her canvases. There is a quite fine wood carving of a Madonna which seems to be centuries old and in the wall spaces looking at audience are great, dim canvases—copies by some former tenant left probably in lieu of rent—of Sargent's Lord Ribblesdale and Mme. X.

Whether it is due to the amenable spirit of the present incumbent or because they are relaxed in the democracy of art, these oddments of the creative spirit do not suggest disharmony. The room is warm, musty, with restful shadows and limpid lights. The enormous leaded window on the right, though some of its members are patched and cracked, gleams in the descending twilight with an opalescent light; even the copper cylinder of the fire extinguisher and its attendant axe, visible in the hall, seem to be not so much implements against calamity, as amusing museum-bits cherished from an earlier time. Every school is represented here except the modern. The studio has the mellowness of anachronism.

RETURN TO A COUNTRY HOUSE

Nothing but darkness enters in this room,
Nothing but darkness and the winter night,
Yet on this bed once years ago a light
Silvered the sheets with an unearthly bloom;
It was the planet Venus in the west
Casting a square of brightness on this bed,
And in that light your dark and lovely head
Lay for a while and seemed to be at rest.

But that the light is gone, and that no more
Even if it were here, would you be here,—
That is one line in a long tragic play
That has been acted many times before,

And acted best when not a single tear
Falls,—when the mind and not the heart holds sway.

SARA TEASDALE

LIGHTS

When we come home at night and close the door,
  Standing together in the shadowy room,
  Safe in our own love and the gentle gloom,
Glad of familiar wall and chair and floor,

Glad to leave far below the clanging city;
  Looking far downward to the glaring street
  Gaudy with light, yet tired with many feet
In both of us wells up a wordless pity;

Men have tried hard to put away the dark;
  A million lighted windows brilliantly
    Inlay with squares of gold the winter night,
But to us standing here there comes the stark
    Sense of the lives behind each yellow light,
  And not one wholly joyous, proud, or free.

SARA TEASDALE

GRACE BEFORE SLEEP

How can our minds and bodies be
Grateful enough that we have spent
Here in this generous room, we three,
This evening of content?
Each one of us has walked through storm
And fled the wolves along the road;
But here the hearth is wide and warm,
And for this shelter and this light
Accept, O Lord, our thanks to-night.

SARA TEASDALE

Gardening

I SOMETIMES wonder why gardeners—and I've had many
around my house in Nyack—are such misanthropes. The
last full-time gardener I had was in the hands of a
psychiatrist.

There is nothing quite like the sense of achievement one
experiences in a garden. Working around in a garden—creating healthy, sturdy plants—how could you ever get that
mixed up in the head that you'd need a headshrinker?

There are, of course, an awful lot of mishaps in a garden
and there are times of frustration and disappointment to
balance the moments of joy and satisfaction. I know. I come
from a line of gardeners, on my father's side.

I remember when I was little we used to go over to see
Grandfather and Grandmother Brown on a Sunday. And
after I'd paid my respects to the awesome grandmother, I'd
tiptoe out to the back to see whether I could catch Grandfather in one of his interminable conversations with his
flowers. Now Grandfather Brown wasn't crazy. But his

flowers were very real to him. They were his beings, and he had a great paternal feeling for them. He felt so responsible. Well, I'd sneak out to the back and I'd hear him saying to a rosebush, "Now look at that one over there. You've had just as much to eat and drink as that one over there and look at you. You're so small. You're not really trying." Things like that he'd say. He'd mutter and scold and cajole and I would roll around in my hiding place in silent laughter.

His son, my father, was the same sort of almost crazy gardener. The flowers that he grew were real to him too, and he just couldn't bear to have anything happen to them. This has come down to me. Whether it's simply that I have followed an example, or because it actually is in the blood, I don't know. But I have been known, after an opening night, to cart my flowers home and stand on my own two feet for three hours, till morning, not waiting for the reviews, not concerned with how the play went, but concerned with cutting off the end of every rose, taking out the wires that the cruel florist had put in, and giving those flowers a chance to drink and breathe, and getting them all properly put away. And that's the way I am about my flowers in my garden.

Actually, I never got a chance to be a very good and experienced gardener because I just didn't have the time. But as work in the theater requires less of my attention and time, and I am freer for the garden, I am becoming one of those fuddy-dud, slightly potty gardeners that are in my paternal line. Potty or dotty, I love it. Once, some years ago, I had a rosebush. It had been a little wan and I worked on it very hard. I fed it, sprayed it, pruned it, and loved it. Then one day, a beautiful rose came out. I took Charlie to see it and I said, "Look at that rose. I worked and slaved to make that rose good, and it is a good rose, and no Brooks Atkinson or any other drama critic can tell me otherwise." I remember that I also said, "That's for me. I prefer that to going on the stage and working hard and trying to create a performance and then having somebody kick it to pieces. But nobody can argue with me about a flower such as this."

I have never ceased to coddle and work and nurture my garden whenever it's been possible, and not so long ago I had my greatest moment of triumph. Without a gardener I had been working on my rose garden myself. The sweat of my brow had dropped to add salt to the ground, or whatever there is in one's sweat. I had really worked and I didn't have a whole nail on my fingers, because I can't bear to wear gloves. I have to work with my bare hands. All through the spring I had worked in that garden alone and I had made those roses. And then the Nyack Garden Club, of which I am a long-time member, had a rose show, at my house. At the last minute I said, "Why don't I pick some of my own roses to swell the show and make it look bigger." And I won the silver cup.

I had won that silver cup twice before, years ago, when I had a brilliant Italian gardener, but it didn't mean much to me at that time. I just congratulated Freddie and felt good for him and kind of wistfully watched him preen himself. But this time there was no Freddie. This third award was mine alone.

Roses are, of course, my favorites. But I also grow all kinds of perennials, all the accepted charmers—crocuses, tulips, and the rest. And I put down my annuals every year, using the lovely marigolds for borders. But the rose that is a rose is the most satisfying. It's the most demanding, it offers a challenge. And it must be treated with respect.

Also, in my garden I find solitude. I can go out there and say, "No phones, no interruptions, I am busy," and then shut myself off for a little while from the demands of daily living, hearing only the sounds of my garden. Those sounds are curiously amusing, delightful and fascinating. There is a family of mourning doves in one corner of the garden. They moan and moan—a soft and gentle sort of sound that always makes me think of springtime and love being vocalized, of "The Song of Solomon."

Besides the mourning doves there are cardinals, whose songs are as brilliant as their plumage. There are wild canaries in great numbers. And altogether my birds provide me with a wonderful symphony that is never distracting. I can think or dream or, as I have done many, many times, learn the lines of a new play there. Thomas Edward Brown, the nineteenth-century poet, summed up the way I feel about my garden.

> A Garden is a lovesome thing, God wot!
>   Rose plot,
>   Fringed pool,
>   Ferned grot—
>   The veriest school
>   Of Peace; and yet the fool
> Contends that God is not—
> Not God! in Gardens! when the eve is cool?
> Nay, but I have a sign:
> 'Tis very sure God walks in mine.

From THE GARDENER'S YEAR

On the Art of Gardening

While I was only a remote and distracted onlooker of the accomplished work of gardens, I considered gardeners to be beings of a peculiarly poetic and gentle mind, who cultivate perfumes of flowers listening to the birds singing. Now, when I look at the affair more closely, I find that a real gardener is not a man who cultivates flowers; he is a man who cultivates the soil. He is a creature who digs himself into the earth, and leaves the sight of what is on it to us gaping good-for-nothings. He lives buried in the ground. He builds his monument in a heap of compost. If he came into the Garden of Eden he would sniff excitedly and say: "Good Lord, what humus!" I think that he would forget to eat the fruit of the tree of knowledge of good and evil; he would rather look round to see how he could manage to take away from the Lord some barrow-loads of the paradisiac soil. Or he would discover that the tree of knowledge of good and evil has not round it a nice dishlike bed, and he would begin to mess about with the soil, innocent of what is hanging over his head. "Where are you, Adam?" the Lord would say. "In a moment," the gardener would shout over his shoulder; "I am busy now." And he would go on making his little bed.

KAREL CAPEK

FLOWERS

I will not have the mad Clytie,
  Whose head is turned by the sun;
The tulip is a courtly queen,
  Whom, therefore, I will shun:
The cowslip is a country wench,
  The violet is a nun;—
But I will woo the dainty rose,
  The queen of every one.

The pea is but a wanton witch,
  In too much haste to wed,
And clasps her rings on every hand;
  The wolfsbane I should dread;

Nor will I dreary rosemarye,
That always mourns the dead;
But I will woo the dainty rose,
 With her cheeks of tender red.

The lily is all in white, like a saint,
 And so is no mate for me;
And the daisy's cheek is tipped with a blush,
 She is of such low degree;

Jasmine is sweet, and has many loves,
 And the broom's betrothed to the bee;—
But I will plight with the dainty rose,
 For fairest of all is she.

THOMAS HOOD

Charlie read every word in the newspapers and he used to devour all the ads. They intrigued him. He was constantly sending away for things; he fell for those ads. One day he came across an ad inserted by a Rochester nursery announcing that you could buy six fruit trees including a flowering almond at something like $1.69 apiece. We had just moved into our house in Nyack and we were very excited about planting our garden. So, understandably enough, when Charlie saw that ad his eyes popped and he came running to me with his discovery. Certainly the price was amazing because all the trees that were offered, as I recall, were rather special. But what delighted Charlie was the idea of getting a flowering almond. That was the star of the lot—a tree with a flower on it. Trembling with anticipation we sent off our money and waited. I don't know exactly what we really expected. But one day they came, with the regular mail; in a sort of tube that was smaller than what is used for picture calendars. And inside were the six twigs which were our trees. It was an awful letdown—six little twigs. But we planted them with all the proper incantations, and we watched them grow, and in proper time Charlie had his flowering almond.

ALMOND BLOSSOM

Blossom of the almond trees,
April's gift to April's bees,
Birthday ornament of Spring,
Flora's fairest daughterling;
Coming when no flowerets dare
Trust the cruel outer air;
When the royal kingcup bold
Dares not don his coat of gold;
And the sturdy black-thorn spray
Keeps his silver for the May;—
Coming when no flowerets would,
Save thy lowly sisterhood,
Early violets, blue and white,
Dying for their love of light;—
Almond blossom, sent to teach us
That the spring days soon will reach us,
Lest, with longing over-tried,
We die, as the violets died;—
Blossom, clouding all the tree
With thy crimson broidery,
Long before a leaf of green
On the bravest bough is seen;—
Ah! when winter winds are swinging
All thy red bells into ringing,
With a bee in every bell,
Almond bloom, we greet thee well.

EDWIN ARNOLD

ON THE GRASSHOPPER AND CRICKET

The poetry of earth is never dead:
When all the birds are faint with the hot sun,
And hide in cooling trees, a voice will run
From hedge to hedge about the new-mown mead:
That is the Grasshopper's—he takes the lead
In summer luxury,—he has never done
With his delights, for when tired out with fun,
He rests at ease beneath some pleasant weed.
The poetry of earth is ceasing never:
On a lone winter evening, when the frost
Has wrought a silence, from the stove there shrills
The Cricket's song, in warmth increasing ever,
And seems to one in drowsiness half-lost,
The Grasshopper's among the grassy hills.

JOHN KEATS

THE GLORY OF THE GARDEN

Our England is a garden that is full of stately views,
Of borders, beds and shrubberies and lawns and
    avenues,
With statues on the terraces and peacocks strutting by;
But the Glory of the Garden lies in more than meets the
    eye.

For where the old thick laurels grow, along the thin red
    wall,
You will find the tool- and potting-sheds which are the
    heart of all;
The cold-frames and the hot-houses, the dungpits and
    the tanks,
The rollers, carts and drain-pipes, with the barrows and
    the planks.

And there you'll see the gardeners, the men and
    'prentice boys
Told off to do as they are bid and do it without noise;
For, except when seeds are planted and we shout to
    scare the birds,
The Glory of the Garden it abideth not in words.

And some can pot begonias and some can bud a rose,
And some are hardly fit to trust with anything that
    grows;
But they can roll and trim the lawns and sift the sand
    and loam,
For the Glory of the Garden occupieth all who come.

Our England is a garden, and such gardens are not
    made
By singing:—"Oh, how beautiful!" and sitting in the
    shade,
While better men than we go out and start their
    working lives
At grubbing weeds from gravel-paths with broken
    dinner-knives.

There's not a pair of legs so thin, there's not a head so
    thick,
There's not a hand so weak and white, nor yet a heart
    so sick,
But it can find some needful job that's crying to be
    done,
For the Glory of the Garden glorifieth every one.

Then seek your job with thankfulness and work till
    further orders,

If it's only netting strawberries or killing slugs on
  borders;
And when your back stops aching and your hands begin
  to harden,
You will find yourself a partner in the Glory of the
  Garden.

Oh, Adam was a gardener, and God who made him sees
That half a proper gardener's work is done upon his
  knees.
So when your work is finished, you can wash your hands
  and pray
For the Glory of the Garden, that it may not pass away!
And the Glory of the Garden it shall never pass away!

RUDYARD KIPLING

MY WINDOWS

These are my two windows; one
Lets in morning and the sun,
Lets in tranquillity and noon,
Lets in all magic and the moon.

One, looking on my garden, shows
Me miracles: a sudden rose,
A poppy's flame, a tulip's cup,
A lily's chalice lifted up.

Wonder-windows! who could guess
The secret of their loveliness?
Beyond transfigured sky and clod
My two windows show me God.

SISTER M. MADELEVA

IN DESERT PLACES

God has a way of making flowers grow.
He is both daring and direct about it.
If you know half the flowers that I know,
You do not doubt it.

He chooses some gray rock, austere and high,
For garden-plot, trafficks with sun and weather;
Then lifts an Indian paintbrush to the sky,
Half flame, half feather.

In desert places it is quite the same;
He delves at petal-plans, divinely, surely,
Until a bud too shy to have a name
Blossoms demurely.

He dares to sow the waste, to plow the rock.
Though Eden knew His beauty and His power,
He could not plant in it a yucca stalk,
A cactus flower.

SISTER M. MADELEVA

Favorite Scenes

AFTER a long career in the theater, it is natural that, for a variety of reasons, an actor should remember with a special affection certain plays in which he or she appeared. Success, of course, is usually the primary reason for those fond recollections, because success brings with it praise, adulation, and affection, which, aside from financial considerations, are the meat and potatoes on which we performers feed. But success alone may not be the principal reason for happy memories. Sometimes we remember great moments in the plays—scenes in which the actor has known a very special and exalting pleasure, scenes of high drama or comedy that have been satisfying and fulfilling experiences. In the close to two score plays in which I have appeared, there have been seven that have provided me with those moments, with what can be called "favorite scenes." Without listing them in order of preference, I now raise the curtain on them in the order of my appearance in them.

Shortly after my eighteenth birthday and my closing in

Penrod, there was a telegram asking me to see William Gillette about appearing with him in James M. Barrie's *Dear Brutus.* I was wanted for the role of Margaret. I fell in love with the play immediately and, as a matter of fact, its significance and its wonderment have grown on me the more I have lived my life. There are those who are inclined to regard Barrie as a sentimentalist. I do not agree. For me Cynthia Asquith, who was his secretary during the last twenty years of his life, is right when she says the "essential Barrie is not sentimental. The real sentimentalist refuses to face hard facts. Barrie does not. For all his reputed 'softness,' he is no escapist. He faces the most painful truths. The silver coating of his writing covers a hard truth, not to be found in the work of many self-styled realists, who for all their brilliant cynicism, still seem naively to suppose that by derision or scolding they can alter human nature. What could be more 'let's face it' than the message of *Dear Brutus* which is that you can never escape from your nature? Midsummer night magic or no, as you enter the moonlit wood so you will come out of it."

In 1926, eight years after my appearance in *Dear Brutus,* I had the pleasure of undertaking a role in another play by James M. Barrie, that of Maggie Shand in *What Every Woman Knows.* And once again through his own brand of comedy Barrie was stating a basic truth. This time it was about the relationship between a husband and wife. What every women knows is that she must never allow her man to realize that she is helping him, but must allow him to think that it is his own intelligence and ingenuity that are getting him on. In the play, Maggie plays an important part in the successful rise of her husband in Parliament. But she also must see him through an affair she knows he is having with Lady Sybil Lazenby. Maggie is shrewd enough to know that by giving Lady Sybil enough rope she will win back her man, which she does. And she charts a shrewd course that guarantees his re-election to Parliament.

There are many warming moments in *What Every Woman Knows*. One that caught my fancy as well as that of audiences comes rather early. It is the moment when Maggie gives her famous definition of charm.

In all my life in the theater I have never had as many letters as I had about that passage. I have repeatedly been asked to recite that little speech in my public appearances, on radio, and on television. For me, the speech is the culmination of one of the shrewdest, most graceful, and most titillating beginnings of any play I have ever appeared in.

ALICK. What *is* charm, exactly, Maggie?

MAGGIE. Oh, it's—it's a sort of bloom on a woman. If you have it, you don't need to have anything else; and if you don't have it, it doesn't much matter what else you have. Some women, the few, have charm for all; and most have charm for one. But some have charm for none.

I appeared in *Mary of Scotland* in 1933 at the Alvin Theater. It was my first portrayal of an historical character. Maxwell Anderson wrote it for me, though just why he selected me, the shortest actress on the American stage, to portray the tallest queen in history was his secret. Perhaps he just wanted to think of her, and have the world think of her, as a small and helpless woman. Booth Tarkington once told me that there were certain people in history about whom it was difficult to be objective, and Mary Stuart was one of them. He said no man had ever been able to write about her without falling in love with her. I found out later that some men, like Stefan Zweig, managed to do it—and even blasted her. But Max was sentimental and he seemed to approve of her. For my part, I had no sentiment in relation to the role. The play itself was beautiful, and I was fascinated with the subject and the period, as I always am about the past. And, even though I was frightened of the role because of my size, I was and am still grateful for having had a chance at it. When I expressed my concern about my height and said also that I didn't think I had the right quality for the part, Max assured me that I probably *wasn't* right for Mary Stuart, but that I was right for his concept of her. He persuaded me, as a matter of fact, not to read any biographies of Mary. He said, "You're playing a role that I have written. You're not playing that woman, you're playing my version of her. So, don't obscure, don't fuzz up my vision of her by reading other people's."

The play opens with Mary arriving to rule her country, and depicts principally the struggle that went on between her and Elizabeth. Elizabeth, in constant fear of Mary, aware of her beauty as well as her legitimate claim to the throne of England, sets out to destroy her. She uses women's weapons —scandal, intrigue, and spying. And Mary, in defiance, takes up with the Catholic Darnley, a weak and stupid man, by whom she becomes pregnant. Ultimately Elizabeth's plan works. Knox, the fanatical anti-Catholic, rouses the army against Mary. She is captured and placed in custody in England. Which leads to my favorite scene, the moment of confrontation between Elizabeth and Mary, a scene by the way that is purely apocryphal, since the two never met. Indeed, from what I understand, Mary did desire a meeting with Elizabeth after she had been thrown into jail. But Elizabeth never wished to face up to such an interview. Perhaps she

With my mother, Catherine Hayes Brown

Me, age 1

Grandmother Hayes in her wedding
dress

Grandfather Hayes

My father and me—when I was 7

With John Drew in *The Prodigal Husband*

With William Gillette
in *Dear Brutus*

Bab

Viola in *Twelfth Night*

With James (at 4) and Mary (at 12)

Jamie, age 7

Me among the perennials, Nyack

In my Nyack living room with Hoopla, 1960

BUD JOHNSON

HERB BREUER

My own white magnolia tree

was stricken by the idea that she had been forced to im-
prison her cousin, or perhaps she feared that Mary would
charm her as she had so many others. But Max, taking a
playwright's liberty, had them meet, and the meeting is a
superb scene—a great statement of the triumph of the spirit
over all vicissitudes. It helped make the play a tremendous
success. In the Greek tragedies it was an accepted fact that
man's destiny was preordained. But it was not the tragedy
that befell man that was the dramatist's concern—it was the
way man met that tragedy, how he rose to the challenge of
life and the challenge of failure, and how he wrestled with
these that made those plays soar. And that is what Max was
trying to do in *Mary of Scotland*. He wanted to show how
Mary rose above her fate.

> MARY. Elizabeth—I have been here a long while
> Already—it seems so. If it's your policy
> To keep me—shut me up—. I can argue no more—
> No—I beg now. There's one I love in the north,
> You know that—and my life's there, my throne's there,
>   my name
> To be defended—and I must lie here darkened
> From news and from the sun—lie here impaled
> On a brain's agony—wondering even sometimes
> If I were what they said me—a carrion-thing
> In my desires—can you understand this?—I speak it
> Too brokenly to be understood, but I beg you
> As you are a woman and I am—and our brightness falls
> Soon enough at best—let me go, let me have my life
> Once more—and my dear health of mind again—
> For I rot away here in my mind—in what
> I think of myself—some death-tinge falls over one
> In prisons—
>   ELIZABETH. It will grow worse, not better. I've known
> Strong men shut up alone for years—it's not

Their hair turns white only; they sicken within
And scourge themselves. If you would think like a queen
This is no place for you. The brain taints here
Till all desires are alike. Be advised and sign
The abdication.

  MARY. Stay now a moment. I begin to glimpse
Behind this basilisk mask of yours. It was this
You've wanted from the first.

  ELIZABETH. This that I wanted?

  MARY. It was you sent Lord Throgmorton long ago
When first I'd have married Bothwell. All this while
Some evil's touched my life at every turn.
To cripple what I'd do. And now—why now—
Looking on you—I see it incarnate before me—
It was your hand that touched me. Reaching out
In little ways—here a word, there an action—this
Was what you wanted. I thought perhaps a star—
Wildly I thought it—perhaps a star might ride
Astray—or a crone that burned an image down
In wax—filling the air with curses on me
And slander; the murder of Rizzio, Moray in that
And you behind Moray—the murder of Darnley, Throg-
  morton
Behind that too, you with them—and that winged
  scandal
You threw at us when we were married. Proof I have
  none
But I've felt it—would know it anywhere—in your eyes—
There—before me.

  ELIZABETH. What may become a queen
Is to rule her kingdom. Had you ruled yours I'd say
She has her ways, I mine. Live and let live
And a merry world for those who have it. But now
I must think this over—sadness has touched your brain.
I'm no witch to charm you, make no incantations;
You came here by your own road.

MARY. I see how I came.
Back, back, each step the wrong way, and each sign
    followed
As you'd have me go, till the skein picks up and we stand
Face to face here. It was you forced Bothwell from me—
You there, and always. Oh, I'm to blame in this, too!
I should have seen your hand!
    ELIZABETH. It has not been my use
To speak much or spend my time—
    MARY. How could I have been
Mistaken in you for an instant?
    ELIZABETH. You were not mistaken.
I am all women I must be. One's a young girl,
Young and harrowed as you are—one who could weep
To see you here—and one's a bitterness
At what I have lost and can never have, and one's
The basilisk you saw. This last stands guard
And I obey it. Lady, you came to Scotland
A fixed and subtle enemy, more dangerous
To me than you've ever known. This could not be borne,
And I set myself to cull you out and down,
And down you are.
    MARY. When was I your enemy?
    ELIZABETH. Your life was a threat to mine, your throne
to my throne,
Your policy a threat.
    MARY. How? Why?
    ELIZABETH. It was you
Or I. Do you know that? The one of us must win
And I must always win. Suppose one lad
With a knife in his hand, a Romish lad who planted
That knife between my shoulders—my kingdom was
    yours.
It was too easy. You might not have wished it.
But you'd take it if it came.
    MARY. And you'd take my life

And love to avoid this threat?

ELIZABETH. Nay, keep your life.
And your love, too. The lords have brought a parchment
For you to sign. Sign it and live.

MARY. If I sign it
Do I live where I please? Go free?

ELIZABETH. Nay, I would you might,
But you'd go to Bothwell, and between you two
You might be too much for Moray. You'll live with me
In London. There are other loves, my dear.
You'll find amusement there in the court. I assure you
It's better than a cell.

MARY. And if I will not sign
This abdication?

ELIZABETH. You've tasted prison. Try
A diet of it.

MARY. And so I will.

ELIZABETH. I can wait.

MARY. And I can wait. I can better wait than you.
Bothwell will fight free again. Kirkaldy
Will fight beside him, and others will spring up
From these dragon's teeth you've sown. Each week that
    passes
I'll be stronger, and Moray weaker.

ELIZABETH. And do you fancy
They'll rescue you from an English prison? Why,
Let them try it.

MARY. Even that they may do. I wait for Bothwell—
And wait for him here.

ELIZABETH. Where you will wait, bear in mind.
Is for me to say. Give up Bothwell, give up your throne
If you'd have a life worth living.

MARY. I will not.

ELIZABETH. I can wait.

MARY. And will not because you play to lose. This
    trespass

Against God's right will be known. The nations will
  know it,
Mine and yours. They will see you as I see you
And pull you down.
    ELIZABETH. Child, child, I've studied this gambit
Before I play it. I will send each year
This paper to you. Not signing, you will step
From one cell to another, step lower always,
Till you reach the last, forgotten, forgotten of men,
Forgotten among causes, a wraith that cries
To fallen gods in another generation
That's lost your name. Wait then for Bothwell's rescue.
It will never come.
    MARY. I may never see him?
    ELIZABETH. Never
It would not be wise.
    MARY. And suppose indeed you won
Within our life-time, still looking down from the heavens
And up from men around us, God's spies that watch
The fall of great and little, they will find you out—
I will wait for that, wait longer than a life,
Till men and the times unscroll you, study the tricks
You play, and laugh, as I shall laugh, being known
Your better, haunted by your demon, driven
To death, or exile by you, unjustly. Why,
When all's done, it's my name I care for, my name and
  heart,
To keep them clean. Win now, take your triumph now,
For I'll win men's hearts in the end—though the sifting
  takes
This hundred years—or a thousand.
    ELIZABETH. Child, child, are you gulled.
By what men write in histories, this or that,
And never true? I am careful of my name
As you are, for this day and longer. It's not what happens
That matters, no, not even what happens that's true,

But what men believe to have happened. They will
      believe
The worst of you, the best of me, and that
Will be true of you and me. I have seen to this.
What will be said about us in after-years
By men to come, I control that, being who I am.
It will be said of me that I governed well,
And wisely, but of you, cousin, that your life,
Shot through with ill-loves, battened on lechery, made
      you
An ensign of evil, that men tore down and trampled.
Shall I call for the lord's parchment?
      MARY. This will be said—?
But who will say it? It's a lie—will be known as a lie!
      ELIZABETH. You lived with Bothwell before Darnley
      died,
You and Bothwell murdered Darnley.
      MARY. And that's a lie!
      ELIZABETH. Your letters, my dear. Your letters to Both-
well prove it.
We have those letters.
      MARY. Then they're forged and false!
For I never wrote them!
      ELIZABETH. It may be they were forged.
But will that matter, Mary, if they're believed?
All history is forged.
      MARY. You would do this?
      ELIZABETH. It is already done.
      MARY. And still I win.
A demon has no children, and you have none,
Will have none, can have none, perhaps. This crooked
      track
You've drawn me on, cover it, let it not be believed
That a woman was a fiend. Yes, cover it deep,
And heap my infamy over it, lest men peer
And catch sight of you as you were and are. In myself

I know you to be an eater of dust. Leave me here
And set me lower this year by year, as you promise,
Till the last is an oubliette, and my name inscribed
On the four winds. Still, STILL I win! I have been
A woman, and I have loved as a woman loves,
Lost as a woman loses. I have borne a son,
And he will rule Scotland—and England. You have no
    heir!
A devil has no children.
    ELIZABETH. By God, you shall suffer
For this, but slowly.
    MARY. And that I can do. A woman
Can do that. Come, turn the key. I have a hell
For you in mind, where you will burn and feel it,
Live where you like, and softly.
    ELIZABETH. Once more I ask you,
And patiently. Give up your throne.
    MARY. No, devil.
My pride is stronger than yours, and my heart beats
    blood
Such as yours has never known. And in this dungeon,
I win here, alone.
    ELIZABETH. *(Turning)*
Goodnight, then.
    MARY. Aye, goodnight.

    (ELIZABETH *goes to the door, which opens before*
    her. She goes out slowly. As the door begins to close
    upon her MARY *calls)*

Beaton!
    ELIZABETH. *(Turning)*
You will not see your maids again,
I think. It's said they bring you news from the north.
    MARY. I thank you for all kindness.

    (ELIZABETH *goes out.* MARY *stands for a moment in*
    thought, then walks to the wall and lays her hand
    against the stone, pushing outward. The stone is

cold, and she shudders. Going to the window she sits again in her old place and looks out into the darkness)

CURTAIN

When Gilbert Miller sent me *Victoria Regina* by Laurence Housman, I let the manuscript lie around for weeks without giving it notice. Those two words on the title page frightened and crushed me. *Victoria Regina*—it sounded so pompous, it sounded like everything that I didn't want to get mixed up in. During that time a friend asked me what I was reading for next season. I told him that Gilbert had sent me *Victoria Regina*. He looked at me and said, "What does that mean?" and when I replied, "Queen Victoria," he said, "Oh, how dark brown!" And this is the way I felt. Then one day Gilbert called and asked, "Have you read it—if you haven't you must at once because I'm going to lose my rights to this. There's some kind of hassle going on and it's imperative that you read it."

Indeed, I had been rude to a dear and trusted friend. So I picked it up and since it was spring and a beautiful day I went out into the garden to read it. I was sitting there, reading the play, when I heard the voices of neighbors, some Nyack ladies coming down to view the garden. I had gotten about half through the manuscript and had become riveted to it. I was so scared that my visitors would break this tremendous rapport between me and my play that I looked around wildly for a place to hide. There is a little bathhouse at the end of our swimming pool—it's very dark, a little wooden thing that's pretty enough on the outside but it sure isn't a place in which to sit cozily and read a play. But I dashed into that because I couldn't make it up to the house without running into those women. And I huddled there. I could hear their voices saying to the gardener, "Where is Mrs. MacArthur?" and so on. And the poor gardener, who had not seen my retreat, kept saying incredulously, "Well, Mrs. MacArthur was here a minute ago." And so, locked in that little bathhouse, sitting there on the floor because there is no chair in there, I finished *Victoria Regina*. Everything about the play seemed so wonderful. I felt that I had a great deal in common with that queen. According to Mr. Housman, and I'm sure according to fact, Queen Victoria was miscast by life. She was meant by nature and her makeup to be a little German Frau, to raise a large family, and to dote on her husband. Yet this little Hausfrau was a queen—the greatest queen of the largest empire in the world, the most important monarch of the world. It is always so extraordinary and so exciting to me to see someone rise to a role for which he is not properly suited. And this she did. She quit just once on it, after Albert's death, and that was because she was primarily and completely a loving wife and a stern mother. A breeder. But I don't think she really cared for the children as much as she did for Albert. There had been several men before him—she was quite susceptible— but when she really fell in love with Albert there could be no other. When he died, she wavered. And she retired from public view. Only Disraeli, by flattery, could lure her out.

As I have said, I loved the play and agreed to do it. But I was scared of doing the old queen. I didn't know how to play that kind of old lady. She was rather fat and pompous and choleric in the last scenes. There were thirty-two vignettes in the original script, and, of these, nine had been selected to be performed, the last three dealing with the aging queen. I just couldn't conceive of being able to play those scenes. Consequently I convinced myself that the play really ended with Albert's death and that it would really be wrong to continue after that. I said to myself this was the love story of a little German princess and she had a fine German prince and we mustn't try to make anything else out of it. Of course I was wrong in every way. But at the time I was aflame with conviction and I spoke to Gilbert Miller about it. He shrugged and said, "If you feel that way, maybe it would be better if you talked to Housman."

Maybe Gilbert knew what he was doing when he agreed to pay my expenses to England to see Housman. I never met such a bullheaded person in my life. Thank goodness he was. When I argued that the play should end with Albert's death because that was the end of the great love story, and that was what the whole play was about and the rest was just tacked on, he wouldn't even discuss it with me. Those last scenes were his reason for writing the play. He brushed me aside. The play had to be done with them or not at all. He behaved like an old bully, a road-company Shaw. So back home I went, defeated and desperate.

Through the rehearsal period I struggled with the old queen. We were playing in Baltimore and I still had not found her. I was awful, like an amateur in a high-school production. I didn't know what to do. I was in a panic, blinded and confused. Then it happened. One night, as I lay in bed my Graddy Hayes marched across my vision. There she was and there was Victoria. She settled down inside of me and took over. My Grandmother Hayes had been a devotee of Victoria. When I was a child, she used to describe Victoria's wedding procession. She had been in the crowd on the curb in London to cheer as the Queen went by. Later, as an old lady, she began to affect the style of Queen Victoria. The Queen died when I was a year old, but for ten years after that my grandmother wore the bonnet with the black egret that was high Victorian fashion, and conducted herself like her idol. I couldn't dissociate Victoria Regina in her scenes as the old lady from my Grandmother Hayes. I never saw anything but my Graddy in my mind's eye every night I played the part. And that was more than a thousand times.

When ex-Queen Ena of Spain visited America and saw the play, I went to have tea with her. "How," she asked, "did you ever learn my grandmother's every mannerism, gesture, idiosyncrasy of behavior and speech? How?" I didn't tell her I was just doing my grandmother. It may have been a far cry from the imperial Queen Victoria. Yet they were simply two old ladies with the same inner spirit. Using one made the other come alive.

Of course, the final scene became for me one of the high points of my career. And I know it is among the most vividly remembered by those who saw it.

The Queen has gone through her sorrows as well as the battles she has had to wage within herself to overcome her weaknesses. She has known her moments of despair and heartbreak, along with the ecstasy of her love for Albert, and she has had to learn how to go on alone after his death. A simple woman, she has done her job to the best of her ability, and I guess there's no more impressive achievement in the world.

Now it is June 20, 1897, and she has just experienced the culminating triumph of her reign—the Diamond Jubilee celebration that marked the date of her accession to the throne. Lifted into her carriage—an open carriage—she has ridden through the streets bowing to her people who have come to love her as one loves a grandmother. You know, if you live

long enough people do overlook your faults a bit. She's come
home. The scene is Buckingham Palace where more than
fifty of her direct descendants, who included most of the
crowned heads of Europe, have gathered. She's exhausted,
but the cheers from outside the Palace can still be heard.
She knows that she must not disappoint those subjects because her greatest gratification that day has been the realization that her people love her, that they appreciate what
she has tried to do for them.

PRINCESS. Won't you go and rest now, Mamma?

THE QUEEN. Not yet. . . . That cheering that I hear
means that my dear people are expecting to see me
again. I must try not to disappoint them.

PRINCESS. It would be nice if you could, Mamma. You
think you can?

THE QUEEN. Yes, but I can't get up. I must go as I am.
Have the windows opened.

(*The windows are opened by the Footmen; the
cheering swells.*)

THE QUEEN. Yes, but over the balustrade, they will not
be able to see me. I must be raised. Tell them to bring
in the sliding dais.

HIS ROYAL HIGHNESS. It is already there in position,
Mamma.

THE QUEEN. Really! How thoughtful! (*And so, when
the window is opened, the sliding dais is let down from
without into the windowframe. While this is being done
with quiet efficiency by the well-trained Footmen, the
QUEEN continues speaking*) Then, now, will you, Bertie,
and some of the others go out, and let them know that I
am coming? Not too many, just a few. (*So six members
of the Royal Family go out on to the balcony, and the
cheering grows louder. THE QUEEN, seeing that the dais*

*is now in position, makes a gesture of command, and
the chair, slowly propelled, mounts the ramp prepared
for it, and passes into the balcony. Immediately the
cheering becomes tremendous, and would go on without
abatement for much longer than exhausted old human
nature can allow.* THE QUEEN *gives the signal for retirement; the chair is withdrawn, and backs into its former
central position, and the Royal Family retire, bowing,
from the public gaze. The dais is lifted, the window is
closed again.*)

THE QUEEN. It's very gratifying, very, to find—after all
these years that they do appreciate all that I have tried
to do for them—for their good, and for this great Country
of ours. We have been so near together today—they and
I: all my dear people of England, and Scotland—*and*
Ireland, and the dear Colonies, and India. From all
round the world I have had messages. Such loyalty—
such devotion! Most extraordinary! Tell Mr. Chamberlain how very much I approve of all the arrangements
he made for the proper representation of all parts of my
Empire in the Procession. Everything so perfectly in
order. Most gratifying! . . . Well, I must go now and
rest, or I shall not be able to take my place at dinner
tonight, and that would never do! . . . So happy! . . . As
we were coming back—you were in front, Bertie, so
perhaps you didn't see—it was just by Hyde Park
Corner, there was a great crowd there; and a lot of rough
men—of course it ought not to have happened, but it
didn't matter—broke right through the lines of the police
and troops guarding the route; and they ran alongside
the carriage, shouting and cheering me. And I heard
them say: "Go it, Old Girl! You've done it well! You've
done it well!" Of course, very unsuitable—the words; but
so gratifying! And oh, I hope it's true! I hope it's true!
. . . Hark! They are still cheering. . . . Albert! Ah! if only
you could have been here!

(*And, having said her say, the great, wonderful, little old Lady gives the signal to her Attendants, and is wheeled slowly away.*)

Early in the Second World War, during the summer of 1940, when, as someone has said, this country was pretending to be neutral, I had gotten myself all steamed up with righteous feelings about our need to sell fifty old destroyers to Great Britain. The idea had created quite a controversy throughout the country. Under the influence of Charlie and Robert E. Sherwood, who had enlisted in the campaign to awaken their fellow citizens to the Nazi threat, I got to making speeches on the beaches at Rye, N.Y., and elsewhere. I had plenty of fervor, though I don't think I fitted the role very well because one day when I made a speech from a lifeguard's platform in Far Rockaway, some of those bathers let me know that they doubted my competence to advise them. "Who do you think you are? Queen Victoria?" one of them jeered—and just about ended that session.

It was then that Maxwell Anderson of the Playwrights Company came around with *Candle in the Wind.* It was a play with a message. Max was hoping to arouse the country to the fact that the Nazis were murdering Europe while we were standing aside and letting it happen. Bob Sherwood, also a member of the Playwrights Company, told me the play was going to help the world, and the Theater Guild was anxious to co-produce it. Alfred Lunt said he would direct it, and so for the first time in my life I agreed to do a play not because I fell in love with it or the character I was to portray, but because it had a specific purpose, a message.

We were all emotionally involved in that play, everyone except my Charlie, who kept saying you can't help the world with a bad play. But we went forging ahead and we met disaster. Ironically, the only character in the play in whom the few who came to the theater had any interest was the Nazi officer. He was a man of wit, cleverness, and cunning, and the audience, what there was of an audience, preferred him to all those righteous people who were crawling around. So that was the terrible result of my effort to do a play for a purpose other than devotion to the play itself.

When *Candle in the Wind* folded, Charlie said, "If you want to get a message to the public, if you want to tell us that we are in trouble and that we had better get ourselves out of it, then the best way is to encourage us, to inspire us by telling us about a time before when we were in a hell of a fix and got out of it." He began looking through an encyclopedia, and when he came to Harriet Beecher Stowe he said, "This is your story, and this is your character, the pivotal character." He and I worked for a long time on a synopsis, and then I finally ended up doing it myself because Charlie had gone to other things.

I sent it to Bob Sherwood, who was down in Washington writing speeches. He didn't respond, and after a long wait with no word I felt a little ashamed. I figured that what I had written must have been pretty terrible. Curiously enough, at that point Gilbert Miller informed me that a play about Harriet Beecher Stowe had been written by a husband-and-wife team, Florence Ryerson and Colin Clements, and that it was going to have a tryout on the campus of Syracuse University. Gilbert, Charlie, and I flew up there to see it. We were very much impressed with it and bought it on the spot. We went back to New York late that night, like old flies dragging ourselves home, but happy because we had found a play.

About a week after Gilbert announced that we would do

the play, there was a letter from Bob Sherwood saying, "I have finished the first act of the play based on your outline and I am well into the second and I have shown it to my agent who thinks it is one of the best things I have ever done. How have you done this to me?" Well, I couldn't have been more shocked, or more horrified. I even went so far as to ask the Clementses what I should do. I showed them the letter and they nearly died. Gilbert encouraged me to go on with the play we had. He pointed out that Bob was apt to get off on some other project. He said that Bob was deeply involved with the war and committed to President Roosevelt. Gilbert also reminded us that he was a slow writer and might, as a matter of fact, never finish the rest of the play. So we went ahead.

The play opened on March 3, 1943, at Henry Miller's Theater, directed by Elia Kazan. In three acts it covers a little more than thirty years in the life of Mrs. Stowe, beginning in the 1830's when she arrived in Cincinnati as a young bride and ending in July 1863 in the Stowe mansion in Andover, Mass., after she has been to Washington to see President Lincoln.

The play describes the reactions to her book, *Uncle Tom's Cabin*, which she wrote out of passionate conviction. She has been under constant fire for that book to the point of having mobs marching on her home. In addition, she has to endure family troubles and tragedy. The final scene, which is my favorite, shows her back home after her trip to Washington, where she had been summoned by President Lincoln. The storm over the book has now subsided and she has been permitted some peace, and now outside her home there is a crowd waiting to hear her report of her journey. There is a rising clamor of voices demanding that she come to the window, show herself, and tell of the trip. She is weary and her spirits are a little limp, and she is reluctant. But her family feels she must do it, so she goes to the French doors leading to the garden. She is helped onto a hassock by her husband. The crowd applauds. She smiles a greeting.

HARRIET. I'm sorry. I'm afraid I am not like Topsy—I have never "just growed." (*The crowd chuckles*) I never realized that so strongly as at the White House when I met our President. When I stepped forward and put my hand in his great prairie of a palm I became as a grasshopper in my own eyes. (*Another murmur of amusement from the crowd*) You know, he is a tall man, very tall, and a plain man, at first sight, but when he smiles—oh, then he becomes Father Abraham!

CROWD. What did he say to you, Mrs. Stowe? What did Mr. Lincoln tell you?

HARRIET. What did he say? Well, first he led me over by the window, then he said, "So you are the little woman who made this great war." Two weeks ago, when I went from among you to the bedside of my son, that would have been an unbearable accusation, for I took with me a heart full of bitterness and doubt. One hour with our President has lifted my spirits and endowed me with new strength. He has made me see that this war, which seems so final to us now, is but one small pattern in a vast tapestry of struggle. Since the dawn of history there have always been tyrants, great and small, who seized upon and enslaved their fellow men. But, equally always, there have been noble souls who bravely and gladly gave their lives for the eternal right of man to liberty. The hope of today lies in this: That we, as a people, are no longer willing to accept these tyrants, and the world they make, without question. We are learning that a world which holds happiness for some but misery for others cannot endure. (*She pauses*) Yes, that is our hope. Our danger is this: When the conflict is finished and war-weariness has set in, we may be tempted to forget, to slip back into the old ways. Then, and then only, will our sons have died in vain. Then will the battle have to be fought again, and, perhaps, yet again. A day will come when this, our little life, will be ended. All will be gone. All who raged, all who threatened; the weaklings who yielded; the men who, like our President, stood and bore infamy and scorn for the truth. Yes, life will be over, but eternity will never efface from our souls whether we did well or ill, fought bravely, or failed like cowards, whether at the end, we could say, with truth, "I have fought the good fight. . . . I have kept the faith." (*She pauses—then adds softly*) For mine eyes have seen the glory——

VOICE (*singing off stage*)—"Of the coming of the Lord. . . ."

VOICES (*off stage*) "He is trampling out the vintage Where the grapes of wrath are stored. . . .

(*First* CALVIN, *then the others in the room take up the song*)

He hath loosed the fateful lightning
Of His terrible swift sword;
His truth is marching on.
Glory! Glory! Hallelujah!
Glory! Glory! Hallelujah!
Glory! Glory! Hallelujah!
His truth is marching on."

CURTAIN

The Skin of Our Teeth was hot off the typewriter when Thornton Wilder telephoned me and said, "I have a new play that I want you to do." Any actress would just drop dead at the idea of Thornton Wilder phoning and I almost did. I was thrilled. He sent me the script, and, when I finished reading it, I went into Charlie's study and said, "It isn't possible. It just can't happen twice to an actress, but this role, this Mrs. Antrobus, is even greater than Victoria. She's the eternal mother, wife, homemaker, and thorn in the side of the world." I was overwhelmed and I phoned Thornton and went on and on blabbing to him about how I loved the play and the role, and finally after a good deal of conversation—the two of us were almost breathless—I said, "And who's going to play my husband?" There was a deathly moment of silence and then Thornton said, "I didn't mean for you to play Mrs. Antrobus. I meant you to play Sabina." I said, "Thornton, my love, I couldn't possibly play that. I couldn't even be one femme fatale, much less the quintessence of all femmes fatales throughout history. I couldn't do it. I'd ruin your beautiful play." He said, "I don't want it played that way, I want it played as an innocent." And I said, "Well, I know that—your writing does indicate that, but still there has to be that quality, there has to be that little sense of ravishment somewhere in that woman. She has to have that sort of animal appeal, but I can't do that. I can't be Sabina. Why can't I be Mrs. Antrobus? That's why I thought you sent me the script." And Thornton said, "Well, you can't play Mrs. Antrobus because the Marches have been engaged—Freddie is going to play Mr. Antrobus and Florence is going to be Mrs. Antrobus." I said no to Sabina and then Thornton really went after me. He sicked the producer, Michael Myerberg, on me, and that man was really harsh. Playwrights and producers, you know, don't like actors making up their minds about things. He really was furious. So I finally suggested Tallulah Bankhead for the role. But he said that was out because Thornton and he had discussed Tallulah and Thornton didn't want her. He wouldn't hear of it. I replied that I thought she'd be really great, and I also said I didn't think playwrights ought to be allowed to cast their own plays. Well, this argument went on for days. Every day they'd call me, hoping I'd change my mind. One day Mr. Myerberg called and said that he would offer the play to Tallulah, unless I would change my mind at once. But I simply said, "Good, that's wonderful." He was non-plussed because he really thought that I would relent. Then a day or so later, and I think this was wonderful of Tallulah, she called and said in her own inimitable style, "Darling, they have sent me this script and they've told me that Thornton wanted you but that you had suggested me. Well, darling, I'm going to do it. I don't care who wants me or doesn't want me, or how low I'm in the line. I love this play and this part and I'm going to do it." I thought that was so adult and wonderful because, you know, actresses are supposed to be touchy about those things. Of course, *The Skin of Our Teeth* won a Pulitzer prize, Tallulah made a big hit and I had to wait almost fifteen years to get a chance to play Mrs. Antrobus—that was when the State Department asked me to go to Paris for an international festival, and Mary Martin was Sabina.

My favorite scene is in the last act. Mrs. Antrobus and her girl child have been shut up for seven years in a cellar wait-ing out yet another catastrophe—this one a war in which, of course, Mr. Antrobus and the male child have fought. Once again, the family of man has survived by the skin of its teeth.

MRS. ANTROBUS. George, do I see you limping?

ANTROBUS. Yes, a little. My old wound from the other war started smarting again. I can manage.

MRS. ANTROBUS. (*Looking out of the window*) Some lights are coming on,—the first in seven years. People are walking up and down looking at them. Over in Hawkins' open lot they've built a bonfire to celebrate the peace. They're dancing around it like scarecrows.

ANTROBUS. A bonfire! As though they hadn't seen enough things burning.—Maggie,—the dog died?

MRS. ANTROBUS. Oh, yes. Long ago. There are no dogs left in Excelsior.—You're back again! All these years. I gave up counting on letters. The few that arrived were anywhere from six months to a year late.

ANTROBUS. Yes, the ocean's full of letters, along with the other things.

MRS. ANTROBUS. George, sit down, you're tired.

ANTROBUS. No, you sit down. I'm tired but I'm restless. (*Suddenly, as she comes forward*) Maggie! I've lost it. I've lost it.

MRS. ANTROBUS. What, George? What have you lost?

ANTROBUS. The most important thing of all: The desire to begin again, to start building.

MRS. ANTROBUS. Well, it will come back.

ANTROBUS. I've lost it. This minute I feel like all those people dancing around the bonfire—just relief. Just the desire to settle down; to slip into the old grooves and keep the neighbors from walking over my lawn.—Hm. But during the war,—in the middle of all that blood and dirt and hot and cold—every day and night, I'd have moments, Maggie, when I *saw* the things that we could do when it was over. When you're at war you think about a better life; when you're at peace you think about a more comfortable one. I've lost it. I feel sick and tired.

MRS. ANTROBUS. Listen! The baby's crying. I hear Gladys talking. Probably she's quieting Henry again. George, while Gladys and I were living here—like moles, like rats, and when we were at our wits end to save the baby's life—the only thought we clung to was that you were going to bring something good out of this suffering. In the night, in the dark, we'd whisper about it, starving and sick.—Oh, George, you'll have to get it back again. Think! What else kept us alive all these years? Even now, it's not comfort we want. We can suffer whatever's necessary; only give us back that promise.

(*Enter* SABINA *with a lighted lamp.*)

SABINA. Mrs. Antrobus . . .

MRS. ANTROBUS. Yes, Sabina?

SABINA. Will you need me?

MRS. ANTROBUS. No, Sabina, you can go to bed.

SABINA. Mrs. Antrobus, if it's all right with you, I'd like to go to the bonfire and celebrate seeing the war's over. And, Mrs. Antrobus, they've opened the Gem Movie Theatre and they're giving away a hand-painted soup tureen to every lady, and I thought one of us ought to go.

ANTROBUS. Well, Sabina, I haven't any money. I haven't seen any money for quite a while.

SABINA. Oh, you don't need money. They're taking anything you can give them. And I have some . . . some . . . Mrs. Antrobus, promise you won't tell anyone. It's a little against the law. But I'll give you some, too.

ANTROBUS. What is it?

SABINA. I'll give you some, too. Yesterday I picked up a lot of . . . of beef-cubes!

MRS. ANTROBUS. But, Sabina, you know you ought to give that in to the Center downtown. They know who needs them most.

SABINA. Mrs. Antrobus, I didn't make this war. I didn't ask for it. And, in my opinion, after anybody's gone through what we've gone through, they have a right to grab what they can find. You're a very nice man, Mr. Antrobus, but you'd have got on better in the world if you'd realized that dog-eat-dog was the rule in the

beginning and always will be. And most of all now.
In tears.
Oh, the world's an awful place, and you know it is. I
used to think something could be done about it; but I
know better now. I hate it. I hate it.
(*She comes forward slowly and brings six cubes
from the bag.*)
All right. All right. You can have them.

ANTROBUS. Thank you, Sabina.

SABINA. Can I have . . . can I have one to go to the
movies?
(ANTROBUS *in silence gives her one.*)
Thank you.

ANTROBUS. Good night, Sabina.

SABINA. Mr. Antrobus, don't mind what I say. I'm just
an ordinary girl, you know what I mean, I'm just an
ordinary girl. But you're a bright man, you're a very
bright man, and of course you invented the alphabet
and the wheel, and, my God, a lot of things . . . and
if you've got any other plans, my God, don't let me
upset them. Only every now and then I've got to go to
the movies. I mean my nerves can't stand it. But if you
have any ideas about improving the crazy old world, I'm
really with you. I really am. Because it's . . . it's . . .
Good night.
She goes out. ANTROBUS *starts laughing softly with
exhilaration.*

ANTROBUS. Now I remember what three things always
went together when I was able to see things most
clearly: three things. Three things:
He points to where SABINA *has gone out.*
The voice of the people in their confusion and their
need. And the thought of you and the children and this
house. . . . And . . . Maggie! I didn't dare ask you: my
books! They haven't been lost, have they?

MRS. ANTROBUS. No. There are some of them right here. Kind of tattered.

ANTROBUS. Yes.—Remember, Maggie, we almost lost them once before? And when we finally did collect a few torn copies out of old cellars they ran in everyone's head like a fever. They as good as rebuilt the world. (*Pauses, book in hand, and looks up*) Oh, I've never forgotten for long at a time that living is struggle. I know that every good and excellent thing in the world stands moment by moment on the razor-edge of danger and must be fought for—whether it's a field, or a home, or a country. All I ask is the chance to build new worlds and God has always given us that second chance, and has given us (*Opening the book*) voices to guide us: and the memory of our mistakes to warn us.

The Glass Menagerie belongs forever to Laurette Taylor, who gave in it one of the great performances to come out of the wings of a Broadway theater. How I inherited her role of Amanda Wingfield is a sad story in my theater life.

As a young actress, I was one of Laurette's most ardent admirers. She had sort of been my guiding star from early girlhood. There was one blessed season in New York when my matinees were on Wednesdays and hers on Thursdays and I saw about every one of them. I went to see her all the time, as people go to church. I wasn't morbidly worshipful, just exhilarated and magnetized by her. When we became friends and she asked me for my photograph to hang in her apartment, I wrote on it the truth. It was corny, but true. It said: "To Laurette, my guiding star." When she gave me her own photograph years later inscribed, "To Helen, who knew how to follow her star," I was filled with great wonder and a profound sense of completion.

It isn't necessary to dwell on the terrible years of agony that she endured, her recurrent bouts with alcoholism that formed the dark and dreadful interlude before her recovery and return from retirement to one of the most luminous and rewarding triumphs of her career in *The Glass Menagerie.* Her daughter, Marguerite Courtney, has told the story beautifully and with exquisitely tender compassion in the biography, *Laurette.* It was a comeback to make fiction scribblers pause, for no one who beheld her as Amanda can ever forget her incandescent genius. Before coming to Broadway, the play had its premiere in Chicago to such hurrahs as the Second City has rarely heard. The heavens had opened with excitement, and on the second night the Chicago drama critics did something probably unheard of in the long history of the theater. They bought tickets and sat in the second row and cheered at the end and threw flowers upon the stage.

I arrived in Chicago a week after the opening, on tour with *Harriet.* The first Sunday night of my run there I went to see Laurette in *The Glass Menagerie.* The theater was full of trouping actors, who, like me, were not playing that night. We had all read the Sunday papers with the second thoughts of the critics on the smashing triumph of Laurette's and Williams' opening a week before. Theater folk are always happy when a great actor has a success, and when a new playwright crashes through. So we were there full of eager expectations. Now comes my moment of shame. I did not like *The Glass Menagerie.* Laurette, as always, enchanted me —with her smile that was April and her voice that Charlie always said was "full of banjos." As she had done for the past thirty years, she had picked me up and carried me aloft. But not to the point that I could cry for Amanda as everyone else around me was doing. I remember Hildegarde, the chanteuse, sitting in front of me, weeping her way through two of her famous handkerchiefs. But me, I could not squeeze out a tear for the Wingfield family—so sad, so hopelessly estranged from life.

I am contrary about tears. I only cry from admiration or joy. My Aunt Mamie Hayes was exactly the same way. She was a perfectly normal and nice woman, except that she never laughed right out loud at funny moments, only at solemn ones. For instance, at her husband's funeral in Arlington—military and high-degree Masonic. During the solemn ritual of the gentlemen with the high silk hats and little aprons and trowels, she suddenly covered her face with her hands and shook agonizingly. "Don't, Aunt Mamie," I whispered, squeezing her arm. One hand came a bit away from the face and one dry eye winked at me reassuringly. The poor woman was shaking with laughter.

In life I have a large sympathy for the lost ones and a sob story finds me a patient listener—but that is private. A public exhibition of the same, however brilliantly written, embarrasses me. I thrill to the fierce pain of O'Neill or the protest of Arthur Miller, or the hilarious scorn of Albee, but some flaw in my makeup has deprived me of response to the spiritually lame and halt in drama.

So there I was, ashamed, castigating myself as I was being swept back to Laurette Taylor's dressingroom amid the tear-soaked crowd. I was so ashamed of how I was feeling that I wouldn't have told the truth under torture. And torture was only a little away, for, after letting everyone rave for a decent period, Laurette threw them all out, sat me down facing her squarely and challenged me, "Come on now, how do you really feel?" This was my moment of truth and I muffed it. Had I told my beloved friend that as always her magic had transported me but I would have to be excused from admiring the play, I should have, in those few

words, saved myself a lot of pain, frustration, and precious
time. Time must be spent with discretion when you are late
on in a career. I couldn't know that night in Chicago that
my cowardly lie was going to trap me into playing Amanda
in twenty-nine countries in two hemispheres. So I let loose
with a flow of tears and superlatives that thrilled both
Laurette and me. It sent her out to round up the young
playwright and all the cast so they could hear me, too. After
that, we repaired, along with Tony Ross and Tennessee
Williams, to a Clark Street bar that Laurette particularly
favored for her one (that was all) after-theater drink, and
there I continued my performance of rapture—gratified by
the pleasure it was giving her and the young playwright.
That was one of the rare times when I got quite high.

After that we made a habit of visiting the bar after performances whenever we were both free. Sometimes we
would have an early dinner before our performances and
Laurette would allow herself a single cocktail. She'd say that
Hartley, her dead husband, would come down and tap her
on the shoulder and whisper, "No more." She was just fine.

And then, of course, she went on to New York and such
glory. After I closed in *Harriet* and was back home, she came
up to Nyack to spend a few weekends.

Whether or not she had premonitions of her destiny I do
not know. But she kept saying, "If I can't do this play in
London you've got to do it." She never got to London.
Laurette died shortly after the New York run, and I knew
that this play had killed her. As much as she loved it, the
whole effort and struggle of the long run had a terrible effect
on this woman who was walking such a tightrope. When
Audrey Wood, Tennessee Williams' agent, came to me after
Laurette's death and asked me to go into the play—she said
that she knew Laurette wanted me to do it—I wanted to

scream at her "I hate your damn play!" I couldn't get it out
of my heart that Laurette had been sacrificed to it. But by
now I was in the lie so deep I couldn't back out. I played it
in London as she had wanted me to. During the run there I
developed a nerve ailment called fibrositis. Very painful it
was: a kind of acute neuralgia. I couldn't sleep with it and
after two tortured nights I experienced my first fear of self-
destruction. I was carrying on with the performances, and
with no sleep I was in a desperate way. A dear friend, Bunty
Cobb, who with her small son had spent the war years with
us in Nyack, came to my aid. She sat up two nights telling
me funny stories.

Frightened as I was of playing Amanda in London, the
thought of playing her in the United States after Laurette's
luminous performance would have finished me—had it
crossed my mind. Little did I know that the time was to
come when I would be trapped by that trauma.

When I returned from the London engagement the movie
people got after me for Amanda. I managed to evade their
blandishments. Then one night several years later, I had a
call from Jean Dalrymple of the New York City Center,
who was in a state of desperation. She was saying, "Unless you will agree and let me go to the bank tomorrow
and say that I have you to play *The Glass Menagerie* at
the City Center later in the season for two weeks, I can't
borrow—we can't borrow money to pay the opera company's
salaries. We'll have to close the opera because we have no
money to pay the singers. And we have no collateral—we
have nothing to offer the bank to get a loan. But if I can tell
them that you are going to do it, they will give me the
loan." And all I kept thinking as Jean was making her plea
was, "Oh God, why me?" But, when she had finished, I said
yes. Charlie used to say I was the head of the sucker list. But

the City Center is one of our country's proudest achieve-
ments in the performing arts—what with the New York City
Ballet and the opera company which it has developed. In its
early years these two were supported to a degree by the
short season of low-budget drama revivals to which high-
priced stars contributed their services. I couldn't refuse,
of course. So I played Amanda in New York. The production, directed by Alan Schneider, was kindly reviewed by the
New York press, and when the two weeks were over, the New
York City Opera Company was safe for another year. I said
good-bye to Amanda—I thought forever.

It seems, however, that my adventures with Amanda
amount to a haunting. When the late Lawrence Lang-
ner, one of the founders of the Theater Guild, was asked
by the State Department to organize a theater company
for a tour abroad, Lawrence came to me in Nyack and
asked me to play Mrs. Antrobus in *The Skin of Our Teeth*.
I was thrilled. I had waited a long time for that role, as I
have related. But there was a catch. You guessed it.
Lawrence also wanted me to do Amanda again. I was hon-
ored to be asked to go on the tour, and the prospect of playing Mrs. Antrobus, whom I adore, was most exhilarating. So
I rallied from the blow of Amanda and put up a struggle. I
came back at Lawrence with a whole list of roles I would
prefer to play, not to mention a whole battery of arguments
in my support. I said that Arthur Miller really ought to be
represented and I would love to play the mother, Mrs.
Loman, in *Death of a Salesman*. Lawrence paid me no heed.
I argued for O'Neill's *Long Day's Journey into Night*, saying
I would love to play the mother, and Lawrence said, "No,
the play is not a picture of American life; surely we are not
going to advertise a mother taking dope and all that." I con-
ceded the point but persisted in the thought that a repertory

without O'Neill made no sense whatever. Besides, in my prejudiced mind I saw nothing in *The Glass Menagerie* as a portrait of American life that did justice. I argued for Thornton Wilder's *Our Town*, a play of affirmation, a play that you knew in your bones was an American classic. But that was turned back because Lawrence said there really wasn't enough of a role in it for me. Finally, I said, "Look, Lawrence, everyone has seen *The Glass Menagerie*. It's been played in so many countries. It's really old hat." Lawrence then recited how he had seen Chekhov's *The Cherry Orchard* many times but not until the Moscow Art Theater had come to America for the first time and given a performance of the play had he really seen it played as it should be played—by the people of the country to whom it belonged. And that was the virtue of our doing *The Glass Menagerie* abroad.

Well, I lost, because Lawrence was really a lawyer by profession and I was just a poor actress with a shamed face and a prejudice. So, I played *The Glass Menagerie* in twenty-eight or twenty-nine countries—the Near East, Europe, the Scandinavian countries, South America. Although there was nothing in Amanda, or her son Tom, to which I could respond, there was one recompense for the heaviness of heart I had about appearing in the play. That was the beauty of the writing itself, great writing of which America can be justly proud. There is one scene that for me is absolutely beautiful, the one between The Gentleman Caller and the poor, lame Laura. I wasn't on during that interlude and I used to just sit in the wings every night and revel in it—the honesty of it and the poignancy of it. It is the moment when Jim, or The Gentleman Caller, and Laura are alone for the first time, the moment for which Amanda has plotted in the hope of finding a husband for her crippled, withdrawn daughter. But Jim is engaged and all the dreams end. The scene, as presented here, is abridged.

JIM. People are not so dreadful when you know them. That's what you have to remember! And everybody has problems, not just you, but practically everybody has got some problems.

You think of yourself as having the only problems, as being the only one who is disappointed. But just look around you and you will see lots of people as disappointed as you are. For instance, I hoped when I was going to high school that I would be further along at this time, six years later, than I am now. . . .

You know what I judge to be the trouble with you?

Inferiority complex! Know what that is? That's what they call it when someone low-rates himself!

I understand it because I had it, too. Although my case was not so aggravated as yours seems to be. I had it until I took up public speaking, developed my voice, and learned that I had an aptitude for science. Before that time I never thought of myself as being outstanding in any way whatsoever!

Now I've never made a regular study of it, but I have a friend who says I can analyze people better than doctors that make a profession of it. I don't claim that to be necessarily true, but I can sure guess a person's psychology, Laura! (*Takes out his gum.*) Excuse me, Laura. I always take it out when the flavor is gone. I'll use this scrap of paper to wrap it in. I know how it is to get it stuck on a shoe.

Yep—that's what I judge to be your principal trouble. A lack of confidence in yourself as a person. You don't have the proper amount of faith in yourself. I'm basing that fact on a number of your remarks and also on certain observations I've made. For instance that clumping you thought was so awful in high school. You say that you even dreaded to walk into class. You see what you did? You dropped out of school, you gave up an education because of a clump, which as far as I know was practically non-existent! A little physical defect is what you have. Hardly noticeable even! Magnified thousands of times by imagination!

You know what my strong advice to you is? Think of yourself as *superior* in some way!

LAURA. In what way would I think?

JIM. Why, man alive, Laura! Just look about you a little. What do you see? A world full of common people! All of 'em born and all of 'em going to die!

Which of them has one-tenth of your good points! Or mine! Or anyone else's, as far as that goes—Gosh!

Everybody excels in some one thing. Some in many!

All my life I had waited for a chance to do an O'Neill play, and I should have been both flattered and overjoyed when Robert Whitehead, the producer, and Harold Clurman, the director, said they wanted me to play the part of Nora Melody in *A Touch of the Poet*. It is a beautiful role, and through it O'Neill was stating his long, tortured, deep concern for his fellow man. His heart's summation is that there is only one terminal dignity, and that is love. It sounds like a dismal cliché, but O'Neill managed to say it without its sounding like a platitude. His inspiration ruled that Nora be in the background, that her inner strength, her dauntlessness would be embarrassing if it occupied the foreground. Her love for her husband, Con Melody, is absolutely selfless. She is capable of overlooking all his faults—that he is a bully and a faker. And what O'Neill is saying is that the subject of a love is not important. What is important is that one is capable of love. He sums it all up in the line, "What is love?

It's when you don't give a thought for all the ifs and want-tos in the world." I understood that because I saw that in Charlie. He was one of those rare people who had and gave absolute love, and I was its subject. My pride tortured me that I hadn't been able to rise to what I knew was there. Then one day I realized that it didn't matter whether or not I was worthy of it, or even whether or not I had responded to it properly. All that mattered was that he had had it. It was his triumph in his personal life, aside from his career, that he was a spirit who was capable of love. And nothing could shake it.

O'Neill had seen this somewhere in his life, in himself or in someone else. Great artist that he was, he knew that if he ever created a character who had achieved perfect love and who was, therefore, impervious to hurt, pride, or any of life's treasons, he must still show that character, despite his or her core of strength, suffering great sorrow and tragedy. What lured me on about the role was the realization that O'Neill had had the genius to write this character and the good sense not to make her the protagonist. And yet, as much as I wanted to play the role, I said no.

There are times when it is just terrible the way I want to run away from things. The more I love them, the more I crave them in the theater, the more I'm afraid of them. I guess it's that I have some sense of not wanting to damage them or something. I have such respect for these things when they appeal to me that I would just hate to be a party to hurting them. Besides, I'm always haunted by being too small and I told myself you couldn't have a cute Nora. Nora is a great big earthy woman, and I couldn't see myself in the part at all. And also I said I didn't know how to do an Irish brogue, and that's so important, especially through the whole first part of the play.

Six months after I had rejected the script, it came back to me. Bob and Harold still wanted me. So I did something rather unusual in the theater for someone who has been around as long as I have—I insisted that they give me an audition. They didn't want to do it, but I continued to insist. I said, "I want to do it. I want to read this out loud and see just how terrible it is." I'd read the play out loud in my own room, but I didn't know whether I could judge from that. I wanted to see the look on their faces. I really wanted very much to do the role, and I determined now to give myself every chance.

I was appearing then in *Time Remembered*, so we made an appointment for midnight, after the performance. I went up to Bob Whitehead's office, and I had my agent, Lucy Kroll, with me. An actor had been provided to read opposite me, to cue my lines. In addition to Bob and Harold several others were there to hear me. Everyone was very self-conscious except me. But I bet no neophyte ever read for an audition and looked up so quickly and so sharply at the face of the director to see how he was taking it. Everyone was smiling and Harold said, laughing, "That was a terrible reading, but I know you can do the part."

And I did.

A Touch of the Poet takes place in Melody's Tavern, a few miles from Boston, during the summer of 1828. The tavern is owned by Con Melody, an Irishman out of Galway who had been a major in the British Army during the war with the French. Although the truth is that his father had been a moneylender and tenant-squeezer, Con has blotted that past from his memory and has paraded himself as having come from a family of quality. He lords it over the other Irish who come to the tavern, lords it over his poor wife for whom he has nothing but disdain. He keeps a mare which he rides in great style, and dresses himself on occasion in the scarlet uniform of a major in one of Wellington's regiments. He is given to quoting poetry, from Byron and others, and he speaks in a refined English style. Yet the masquerade makes no impression on the Yankee gentry, who regard him and the other Irish in the neighborhood as scum. Con is a drinker. He has led poor Nora, who lacks his wit and manners, a very hard life.

The scene I have selected is the one that comes at the end. Con has discovered that the parents of a young Yankee are opposed to their son's having anything to do with his daughter Sara. They have sent a lawyer to offer money so that Con will move his family away from Massachusetts. Con is enraged. He attires himself in his uniform and goes off to find the Yankee father in order to force him into a pistol duel. But the Yankee will not soil his hands on Con, and the whole adventure turns into a brawling fiasco to which the police are called. Con returns, degraded, all his illusions stripped from him. He means to kill the mare and then himself. But he kills only the mare, realizing that in that act he has killed himself also. No longer will he be the strutting major. He will tend bar like any other man. He will talk again with an Irish brogue. Through it all, Nora dazed and not quite understanding that her husband is dying right before her eyes, does all she can do. She gives him acceptance. The last scene is between Nora and Sara. Con has gone into the bar to drink with the men he has, until now, despised.

NORA. (*Overcome by physical exhaustion again, sighs.*) Don't mind his giving you a slap. He's still quare in his head. But he'll sing and laugh and drink a power av whiskey and slape sound after, and tomorrow he'll be himself again—maybe.

SARA. *(Dully—aloud to herself rather than to her mother.)* No. He'll never be. He's beaten at last and he wants to stay beaten. Well, I did my best. Though why I did, I don't know. I must have his crazy pride in me. *(She lifts her head, her face hardening—bitterly.)* I mean, the late Major Melody's pride. I mean, I did have it. Now it's dead—thank God—and I'll make a better wife for Simon.

> *(There is a sudden lull in the noise from the bar, as if someone had called for silence—then Melody's voice is plainly heard in the silence as he shouts a toast:* "Here's to our next President, Andy Jackson! Hurroo for Auld Hickory, God bless him!" *There is a drunken chorus of answering* "hurroos" *that shakes the walls.*

NORA. Glory be to God, cheerin' for Andy Jackson! Did you hear him, Sara?

SARA. *(Her face hard.)* I heard someone. But it wasn't anyone I ever knew or want to know.

NORA. *(As if she hadn't heard.)* Ah well, that's good. They won't all be hatin' him now. *(She pauses—her tired, worn face becomes suddenly shy and tender.)* Did you hear him tellin' me he loved me, Sara? Did you see him kiss me on the mouth—and then kiss my hair? *(She gives a little, soft laugh.)* Sure, he must have gone mad altogether!

SARA. *(Stares at her mother. Her face softens.)* No, Mother, I know he meant it. He'll keep on meaning it, too, Mother. He'll be free to, now. *(She smiles strangely.)* Maybe I deserved the slap for interfering.

NORA. *(Preoccupied with her own thoughts.)* And if he wants to kape on makin' game of everyone, puttin' on the brogue and actin' like one av thim in there—*(She nods toward the bar.)* Well, why shouldn't he if it brings him peace and company in his loneliness? God pity him, he's had to live all his life alone in the hell av pride. *(Proudly.)* And I'll play any game he likes and give him love in it. Haven't I always? *(She smiles.)* Sure, I have no pride at all—except that.

SARA. *(Stares at her—moved.)* You're a strange, noble woman, Mother. I'll try and be like you. *(She comes over and hugs her—then she smiles tenderly.)* I'll wager Simon never heard the shot or anything. He was sleeping like a baby when I left him. A cannon wouldn't wake him.

> *In the bar, Riley starts playing a reel on his pipes and there is the stamp of dancing feet. For a moment Sara's face becomes hard and bitter again. She tries to be mocking.*

Faith, Patch Riley don't know it but he's playing a requiem for the dead. *(Her voice trembles.)* May the hero of Talavera rest in peace! *(She breaks down and sobs, hiding her face on her mother's shoulder—bewilderedly.)* But why should I cry, Mother? Why do I mourn for him?

NORA. *(At once forgetting her own exhaustion, is all tender, loving help and comfort.)* Don't, darlin', don't. You're destroyed with tiredness, that's all. Come on to bed, now, and I'll help you undress and tuck you in. *(Trying to rouse her—in a teasing tone.)* Shame on you to cry when you have love. What would the young lad think of you?

CURTAIN

Faith and Affirmation

I T is told of the great skeptical philosopher Voltaire that once he and a friend were walking on the street when a religious procession passed them by. To the friend's great astonishment, Voltaire doffed his hat as a sign of reverence. "Monsieur Voltaire," the friend exclaimed, "have you become a religious believer?" "My dear friend," Voltaire answered, "when God and I pass each other we salute, but we do not speak."

I think it is unfortunately true of a great many men and women today that though they believe in God they do not feel the need to speak or, if you will, pray to him. Prayer, a rabbi has said, is a "ladder reaching from earth to heaven, from man to God" and without prayer no religion is truly alive.

I know that we are told that every good thought we have and everything we do that is good is actually in itself a prayer; that everything we do that is imbued with kindness or love for others is our simple and sincere way of telling

God that we are grateful for what good we have from him. I know this is true, but I don't think it is enough. It reminds me of the story of the lazy man who had his secretary or someone else copy a whole lot of prayers for him which he had pinned up on the wall of his bedroom, and, when it was time to pray, he would just point to one and say, "Lord, them's my sentiments."

There is a certain value in the discipline of saying the formal prayers that have been created by inspired men. As an actress I have known the value of discipline since childhood. I have been taught that each performance must be fresh and good and you must never relax or let down. This sense of discipline also comes from my Catholic upbringing. As Rabbi Robert Gordis observed in his *A Faith for Moderns*, "Even if the goal of true communion with God is achieved only intermittently, it justifies the discipline, the routine, even the long periods when the heart is silent though the lips move, when God seems absent though His name is repeated time and again." Gordis continues with a marvelous parable once told by the Rabbi of Rizin.

"In a small village the only watchmaker died, and because the population was small, no new craftsman came to take his place. As time went on, watches and clocks began to lose and gain time, and no accurate timepieces remained. Some villagers accordingly let their watches run down, while others doggedly kept winding theirs each day, though their accuracy left much to be desired. Some time later, a wandering watchmaker came to town, and all the villagers rushed to bring their timepieces for repair. Those watches that had been allowed to run down were beyond repair, for their mechanisms had rusted. The lesson is clear. The spiritual life must be guarded against merely perfunctory exercise, to be sure, but even the routine performance serves as a necessary discipline and the prelude to great moments of exaltation open to every man."

Spontaneous prayers are usually pretty inadequate, it seems to me, when one is asking God for the impossible much of the time—or else thanking Him for making the impossible come to pass. Those prayers usually come out as "God help us" or "Thank God" or "Great God Almighty" or something of that sort. They are perfectly good prayers, of course, and do relieve one. But when the head is cleared it is pleasant, I think, to address God politely as one would any friend of whom one is seeking a favor. I have never felt satisfied with my own made-up prayers. So I very often turn to David, the Poet King, or Paul the Epistler. They are my favorites. They roar and they sing—they never wheedle or whine. They have provided me with sustenance as they have countless others through the ages. Let me give you two specific examples.

When the news came over the radio announcing that D-Day had begun, it was as if that radio had sent me a personal message. I knew at that moment that my husband, Charles MacArthur, must be in that invasion. Only two weeks before, I had seen him off with General William Porter. Neither of them would tell me what their mission was. But I knew that General Porter was Chief of Chemical Warfare, and Charlie was his special assistant. And Charlie had written from London that "lively doings"—which was a favorite phrase of his—were coming up. So, when the news came that we were sending those boats onto the beaches I suspected that he would be in one of them. Knowing my husband, I just didn't think that he could be kept out. And it was true. He and the general weren't in the first wave, they were in the second. But I knew on D-Day that they would be part of it, and I did what so many others in my home town of Nyack did—I ran to church, the Dutch Reformed Church, because I had not yet returned to my own. I wanted to say a prayer. The church was full when I got there, and I took my place in the back. There were several books in the little rack of the bench in front of me, and I picked up the Psalter—David, my ever-present friend in need. I opened the pages and began turning, searching for the 121st Psalm, which begins, "I will raise up my eyes unto the hills, from whence cometh my help." I was going to read that and get strength, because I was pretty scared. And, somehow, as I turned the pages, my eyes stopped over a new one, new that is, to me—the 93rd Psalm:

> The Lord reigneth, he is clothed with majesty; the Lord is clothed with strength, wherewith he had girded himself: the world also is established, that it cannot be moved.
> Thy throne is established of old; thou art from ever-lasting.
> The floods have lifted up, O Lord, the floods have lifted up their voice; the floods lift up their waves.
> The Lord on high is mightier than the noise of many waters, yea, than the mighty waves of the sea.
> Thy testimonies are very sure: holiness becometh thine house, O Lord, for ever.

When I had finished, I knew that by some miracle I had found this one. It had been exactly what I had needed. It was the exact word, like balm to a tortured spirit. It calmed me and settled me and set me walking out of the church with my head high and new courage in my heart. I had received the strength I needed, and I knew then that I would not disgrace Charlie.

There was a time in my life when, like a great number of people since religion began—and that's since man began— I drifted away from formal religion and closeness to God. In the years when it seemed that nothing could ever go wrong I came to think, as William Ernest Henley had writ- ten in his "Invictus," that I was the master of my fate and the "captain of my soul." Everything, it seemed, hap- pened as I had intended it to happen—finding just the right plays and such. It wasn't that I did not believe or that I did not call upon God from time to time. It was simply that I had become sort of careless and took my faith for granted. And then there came the moment of my tragedy. My daughter Mary died. And I felt the desperate need for help—beyond anything that anyone could give me. So, I tried desperately to find my way back to a com- plete acceptance and realization of my identity with God as my friend and my strength. Yet, for a long time I could not make it happen, as I had made so many other things happen in my proud youth. I couldn't get back where I was when I was a child, when I was very young and felt an intimacy with God. I found that I couldn't just say, "Well now, I want faith—come on, where's that faith, it's got to come right in here"—as if I could order faith like you order a good dinner. So there I was for months desperate and in despair, struggling. One night I had been tossing as I had so many other nights before, sleepless. I suddenly sat up and turned on the light, and reached for the Psalter that I'd always had by my bed. I seem to recall that I wanted to read the 93rd Psalm; the one I had found on D-Day. But instead I discovered that I had opened to the 40th. And there it was —in those early dark hours of the morning:

> I waited patiently for the Lord; and he inclined unto me, and heard my cry.

He brought me up also out of an horrible pit, out of the miry clay, and set my feet upon a rock, and established my goings.

And he hath put a new song in my mouth, even praise unto our God: many shall see it, and fear, and shall trust in the Lord.

Blessed is that man that maketh the Lord his trust, and respecteth not the proud, nor such as turn aside to lies.

Many, O Lord my God, are thy wonderful works which thou hast done, and thy thoughts which are to us-ward: they cannot be reckoned up in order unto thee: if I would declare and speak of them, they are more than can be numbered.

Sacrifice and offering thou didst not desire; mine ears hast thou opened: burnt offering and sin offering hast thou not required.

Then said I, Lo, I come: in the volume of the book it is written of me,

I delight to do thy will, O my God: yea, thy law is within my heart.

I have preached righteousness in the great congregation: lo, I have not refrained my lips, O Lord, thou knowest.

I have not hid thy righteousness within my heart, I have declared thy faithfulness and thy salvation: I have not concealed thy loving kindness and thy truth from the great congregation.

Withhold not thou thy tender mercies from me, O Lord; let thy lovingkindness and thy truth continually preserve me.

For innumerable evils have compassed me about: mine iniquities have taken hold upon me, so that I am not able to look up; they are more than the hairs of mine head: therefore my heart faileth me.

Be pleased, O Lord, to deliver me: O Lord, make haste to help me.

Let them be ashamed and confounded together that seek after my soul to destroy it; let them be driven backward and put to shame that wish me evil.

Let them be desolate for a reward of their shame that say unto me, Aha, aha.

Let all those that seek thee rejoice and be glad in thee: let such as love thy salvation say continually, The Lord be magnified.

But I am poor and needy; yet the Lord thinketh upon me: thou art my help and my deliverer; make no tarrying, O my God.

I finished it and greedily reread the lines again and again, especially the first eight verses and the last two. I felt better and I waited patiently from that moment on. I thought that if King David had had his moments of doubt, and if he could be so patient, so could I. And I remembered the lives of the saints. So many of them were involved in a struggle with a faith. They had wavered and returned. And I understood that night that you must have patience. I understood that faith comes of itself, not by straining after it.

I believe I read somewhere that the 23rd Psalm is frequently read at both Jewish and Christian funerals. It was among Charlie's favorites as it has been mine, and it was also cherished by my mother throughout her lifetime. I know it by heart, and it was I who recited it at my mother's grave when we buried her. I stood alone with Charlie and my son Jim beside the grave. I faltered once in that recital, and I remember Charlie steadying me with the pressure of his hand. I read it because I was the only one who ever pleased mother in reading anything, and I knew that she would be unhappy wherever she was if I hadn't. I could imagine her saying, wherever she was, "Why should some totally untalented priest have the best lines while Helen was standing by?"

The Lord is my shepherd; I shall not want.

He maketh me to lie down in green pastures: he leadeth me beside the still waters.

He restoreth my soul: he leadeth me in the paths of righteousness for his name's sake.

Yea, though I walk through the valley of the shadow of death, I will fear no evil: for thou art with me; thy rod and thy staff they comfort me.

Thou preparest a table before me in the presence of mine enemies: thou anointest my head with oil; my cup runneth over.

Surely goodness and mercy shall follow me all the days of my life: and I will dwell in the house of the Lord for ever.

From THE GREEK WAY TO WESTERN CIVILIZATION

Mind and Spirit

Egypt is a fertile valley of rich river soil, low-lying, warm, monotonous, a slow-flowing river, and beyond, the limitless desert. Greece is a country of sparse fertility and keen, cold winters, all hills and mountains sharp cut in stone, where strong men must work hard to get their bread. And while Egypt submitted and suffered and turned her face toward death, Greece resisted and rejoiced and turned full-face to life. For somewhere among those steep stone mountains, in little sheltered valleys where the great hills were ramparts to defend and men could have security for peace and happy

living, something quite new came into the world; the
joy of life found expression. Perhaps it was born there,
among the shepherds pasturing their flocks where the
wild flowers made a glory on the hillside; among the
sailors on a sapphire sea washing enchanted islands
purple in a luminous air. At any rate it has left no trace
anywhere else in the world of antiquity. In Greece
nothing is more in evidence. The Greeks were the first
people in the world to play, and they played on a great
scale. All over Greece there were games, all sorts of
games; athletic contests of every description: races—
horse-, boat-, torch-races; contests in music, where one
side outsung the other; in dancing—on greased skins
sometimes to display a nice skill of foot and balance of
body; games where men leaped in and out of flying
chariots; games so many one grows weary with the list
of them. They are embodied in the statues familiar to
all, the disc thrower, the charioteer, the wrestling boys,
the dancing flute players. The great games—there were
four that came at stated seasons—were so important,
when one was held, a truce of God was proclaimed so
that all Greece might come in safety without fear. There
"glorious-limbed youth"—the phrase is Pindar's, the ath-
lete's poet—strove for an honor so coveted as hardly anything else in Greece. An Olympic victor—triumphing
generals would give place to him. His crown of wild
olives was set beside the prize of the tragedian. Splendor
attended him, processions, sacrifices, banquets, songs
the greatest poets were glad to write. Thucydides, the
brief, the severe, the historian of that bitter time, the fall
of Athens, pauses, when one of his personages has con-
quered in the games, to give the fact full place of honor.
If we had no other knowledge of what the Greeks were
like, if nothing were left of Greek art and literature, the
fact that they were in love with play and played mag-
nificently would be proof enough of how they lived and

how they looked at life. Wretched people, toiling people, do not play. Nothing like the Greek games is conceivable in Egypt or Mesopotamia. The life of the Egyptian lies spread out in the mural paintings down to the minutest detail. If fun and sport had played any real part they would be there in some form for us to see. But Egyptians did not play. "Solon, Solon, you Greeks are all children," said the Egyptian priest to the great Athenian. At any rate, children or not, they enjoyed themselves. They had physical vigor and high spirits and time, too, for fun. The witness of the games is conclusive. And when Greece died and her reading of the great enigma was buried with her statues, play, too, died out of the world. The brutal, bloody Roman games had nothing to do with the spirit of play. They were fathered by the Orient, not by Greece. Play died when Greece died and many and many a century passed before it was resurrected.

To rejoice in life, to find the world beautiful and delightful to live in, was a mark of the Greek spirit which distinguished it from all that had gone before. It is a vital distinction. The joy of life is written upon everything the Greeks left behind and they who leave it out of account fail to reckon with something that is of first importance in understanding how the Greek achievement came to pass in the world of antiquity. It is not a fact that jumps to the eye for the reason that their literature is marked as strongly by sorrow. The Greeks knew to the full how bitter life is as well as how sweet. Joy and sorrow, exultation and tragedy, stand hand in hand in Greek literature, but there is no contradiction involved thereby. Those who do not know the one do not really know the other either. It is the depressed, the gray-minded people, who cannot rejoice just as they cannot agonize. The Greeks were not the victims of depression. Greek literature is not done in gray or with a low palette.

It is all black and shining white or black and scarlet and gold. The Greeks were keenly aware, terribly aware, of life's uncertainty and the imminence of death. Over and over again they emphasize the brevity and the failure of all human endeavor, the swift passing of all that is beautiful and joyful. To Pindar, even as he glorifies the victor in the games, life is "a shadow's dream." But never, not in their darkest moments, do they lose their taste for life. It is always a wonder and a delight, the world a place of beauty, and they themselves rejoicing to be alive in it.

EDITH HAMILTON

From ANDROCLES AND THE LION

THE CAPTAIN. What you are facing is certain death. You have nothing left now but your faith in this craze of yours: this Christianity. Are your Christian fairy stories any truer than our stories about Jupiter and Diana, in which, I may tell you, I believe no more than the Emperor does, or any educated man in Rome?

LAVINIA. Captain: all that seems nothing to me now. I'll not say that death is a terrible thing; but I will say that it is so real a thing that when it comes close, all the imaginary things—all the stories, as you call them—fade into mere dreams beside that inexorable reality. I know now that I am not dying for stories or dreams. Did you hear of the dreadful thing that happened here while we were waiting?

THE CAPTAIN. I heard that one of your fellows bolted, and ran right into the jaws of the lion. I laughed. I still laugh.

LAVINIA. Then you don't understand what that meant?

THE CAPTAIN. It meant that the lion had a cur for his breakfast.

LAVINIA. It meant more than that, Captain. It meant that a man cannot die for a story and a dream. None of us believed the stories and the dreams more devoutly than poor Spintho; but he could not face the great reality. What he would have called my faith has been oozing away minute by minute whilst I've been sitting here, with death coming nearer and nearer, with reality become realler and realler, with stories and dreams fading away into nothing.

THE CAPTAIN. Are you then going to die for nothing?

LAVINIA. Yes: that is the wonderful thing. It is since all the stories and dreams have gone that I have now no doubt at all that I must die for something greater than dreams or stories.

THE CAPTAIN. But for what?

LAVINIA. I don't know. If it were for anything small enough to know, it would be too small to die for. I think I'm going to die for God. Nothing else is real enough to die for.

THE CAPTAIN. What is God?

LAVINIA. When we know that, Captain, we shall be gods ourselves.

GEORGE BERNARD SHAW

GOD'S WORLD

O world, I cannot hold thee close enough!
Thy winds, thy wide gray skies!
Thy mists, that roll and rise!
Thy woods, this autumn day, that ache and sag
And all but cry with color! That gaunt crag
To crush! To lift the lean of that black bluff!
World, world, I cannot get thee close enough!

Long have I known a glory in it all
But never knew I this.

Here such a passion is
As stretcheth me apart. Lord, I do fear
Thou'st made the world too beautiful this year.
My soul is all but out of me—let fall
No burning leaf; prithee, let no bird call.

EDNA ST. VINCENT MILLAY

SWEET AND SOUR

From "AMORETTI"

Sweet is the rose, but grows upon a brier;
Sweet is the juniper, but sharp his bough;
Sweet is the eglantine, but pricketh near;
Sweet is the fir-bloom, but his branches rough;
Sweet is the cypress, but his rind is tough;
Sweet is the nut, but bitter is his pill;
Sweet is the broom-flower, but yet sour enough;
And sweet is moly, but his root is ill:
So every sweet with sour is tempered still.
That maketh it be coveted the more;
For easy things, that may be got at will,
Most sorts of men do set but little store.
   Why then should I account of little pain,
   That endless pleasure shall unto me gain?

EDMUND SPENSER

Even before the late Dudley Digges introduced me to his
fellow Irishman James Stephens, I had been an addict of
Stephens' poetry. The winter of our meeting I saw a great
deal of him. He had been visiting the United States, and
hostesses, of course, besieged him with their invitations. At
one of the parties we spent a good deal of time together, and

he told me an amusing story that I have recounted to friends ever since. It seems that Stephens had lived on the continent for some time, and no doubt in London, too—Irish turncoat that he was—and he decided he'd better return to Ireland and get familiar once more with his roots, reacquainting himself with his people. He took a walking trip across the land, stopping every once in a while and striking up conversation with people he met along the way. He recalled a cottage he had seen. In front of it sat a man with a mop of red hair and a red beard that almost covered his whole face. From between the shaggy red brows and the beard there peered two bright blue eyes. The man was sitting with his chair tilted back against the whitewashed wall of the cottage. Stephens went up to him and tried to draw him out with a lot of questions. But the fellow always answered in monosyllables. Finally, Stephens said, "Tell me, isn't this supposed to be a place of magic, this area? Did you ever see a Pooky?" And the man made his longest speech of that dialogue. "Seen one?" he said. "I'm bothered by 'em."

THE VOICE OF GOD

I bent unto the ground
And I heard the quiet sound
Which the grasses make when they
Come up laughing from the clay.

"We are the voice of God," they said:
Thereupon I bent my head
Down again that I might see
If they truly spoke to me.

But around me everywhere
Grass and tree and mountain were

Thundering in a mighty glee,
"We are the voice of deity."

And I leapt from where I lay,
I danced upon the laughing clay,
And to the rock that sang beside,
"We are the voice of God," I cried.

JAMES STEPHENS

THE WHISPERER

The moon was round,
And as I walked along
There was no sound,
Save where the wind with long
Low hushes whispered to the ground
  A snatch of song.

No thought had I
Save that the moon was fair,
And fair the sky,
And God was everywhere.

JAMES STEPHENS

From THE AMBASSADORS

Live all you can; it's a mistake not to. It doesn't so
much matter what you do in particular, so long as you
have your life. If you haven't had that, what *have* you
had? . . . What one loses one loses; make no mistake
about that. The affair—I mean the affair of life—couldn't,
no doubt, have been different for me; for it's, at the best,
a tin mould, either fluted and embossed, with ornamental excrescences, or else smooth and dreadfully

plain, into which, a helpless jelly, one's consciousness is poured—so that one 'takes' the form, as the great cook says, and is more or less compactly held by it: one lives, in fine, as one can. Still, one has the illusion of freedom; therefore don't be, like me, without the memory of that illusion. I was either, at the right time, too stupid or too intelligent to have it; I don't quite know which. Of course, at present, I'm a case of reaction against the mistake; and the voice of reaction should, no doubt, always be taken with an allowance. But that doesn't affect the point that the right time is now yours. The right time is *any* time that one is still so lucky as to have. You've plenty; that's the great thing; you're, as I say, damn you, so happily and hatefully young. Don't, at any rate, miss things out of stupidity. Of course I don't take you for a fool, or I shouldn't be addressing you thus awfully. Do what you like so long as you don't make *my* mistake. For it was a mistake. Live!"

HENRY JAMES

THE NIGHT IS NOT DARK

They tell of Adam:

How frightened he must have been when, for the first time, he saw the sun disappear, ending the light of day.

It was Adam's first *darkness!*

How could he understand the night, when he had never seen a dawn?

After the splendor of the sun, how astonishingly dark the darkness was; how desperate the long terror of the first fall of night . . . until Adam learned that *day* would come again: that there is order in the universe.

And then Adam could begin to see how much light *remains* in the sky at night: the stars, and their enduring promise of the sun . . .

The returning star of day.

Adam learned *the night is never wholly dark, and no night is endless* . . . even as each of us must learn it in our own times of trouble and of darkness.

The light is never far.

> from an advertisement in the *New York Times* placed by The Jewish Theological Seminary of America

i thank You God for most this amazing

i thank You God for most this amazing
day: for the leaping greenly spirits of trees
and a blue true dream of sky; and for everything
which is natural which is infinite which is yes

(i who have died am alive again today,
and this is the sun's birthday; this is the birth
day of life and of love and wings: and of the gay
great happening illimitably earth)

how should tasting touching hearing seeing
breathing any—lifted from the no
of all nothing—human merely being
doubt unimaginable You?

(now the ears of my ears awake and
now the eyes of my eyes are opened)

E. E. CUMMINGS

O WORLD

O world, thou choosest not the better part!
It is not wisdom to be only wise,

And on the inward vision close the eyes,
But it is wisdom to believe the heart.
Columbus found a world, and had no chart,
Save one that faith deciphered in the skies;
To trust the soul's invincible surmise
Was all his science and his only art.
Our knowledge is a torch of smoky pine
That lights the pathway but one step ahead
Across a void of mystery and dread.
Bid, then, the tender light of faith to shine
By which alone the mortal heart is led
Unto the thinking of the thought divine.

GEORGE SANTAYANA

PIED BEAUTY

Glory be to God for dappled things—
    For skies of couple-color as a brinded cow;
        For rose-moles all in stipple upon trout that swim;
Fresh-firecoal chestnut-falls; finches' wings;
    Landscape plotted and pieced—fold, fallow, and plow:
        And all trades, their gear and tackle and trim.

All things counter, original, spare, strange;
    Whatever is fickle, freckled (who knows how?)
        With swift, slow; sweet, sour; adazzle, dim;
He fathers-forth whose beauty is past change:
        Praise Him.

GERARD MANLEY HOPKINS

Many times through the years I have been invited to read, over television or radio, material that has either been brought to my attention or that I have found in my browsing and enjoyed. The occasions for these readings generally have been anniversaries, testimonials to persons living or recently passed away, or the observance of national or religious holidays. One of these readings took place November 17, 1957, when General Motors presented its fiftieth anniversary show over NBC-TV. I was asked to recite Helen Deutsch's "The White Magnolia Tree," which has become a favorite of mine. As I read it that night I couldn't help feeling that it would be lost amid all the other hoopla of what had been an expensively produced show. But, as soon as I finished reading it, the telephones began ringing. And the following day the station was inundated with mail seeking copies or information on where the poem could be found. Under the pressure of the mounting requests, General Motors had the poem printed in a booklet which it then distributed. I, myself, sent out several hundred.

THE WHITE MAGNOLIA TREE

The year when I was twenty-one
(John that year was twenty-three)
That was the year, that was the spring,
We planted the white magnolia tree.

"This tree," said John, "shall grow with us,
And every year it will bloom anew.
This is our life. This is our love."
And the white magnolia grew and grew . . .

Oh, youth's a thing of fire and ice
And currents that run
Hot and white,
And its world is as bright
As the sun . . .

I was twenty-one . . .

And I wore a plume in my hat, and we went to the movies and wept over "Stella Dallas," and John sang "Moonlight and Roses" (a little off-key, but very nicely really), and we hurried through our crowded days with beautiful plans, boundless ambitions and golden decisions.

There is so much the young heart clamors for; this it must have, and that it cannot live without, and it must be all or nothing, for aren't we the masters of creation?

Oh, valiant and untamed were we,
When we planted the white magnolia tree!

And the white magnolia grew and grew,
Holding our love within its core,
And every year it bloomed anew,
And we were twenty-one no more.

No more untamed, no more so free,
Nor so young, nor so wild and aflame were we.

Dearer to us then grew other things: easy sleep, books, a day's quiet holiday, good talk beside a fire, the beauty of old faces . . .

We have known many things since then: the death of a child and the bitter lesson that a heart which breaks must mend itself again (that it can and must be done), and what loyalty can mean, and how real a word like courage can become, and that solitude can be rich and gratifying and quite different from loneliness . . .

There is so little the serious heart requires: friends, faith, a window open to the world,

pride in work well done, and strength to
live in a world at war and still maintain
the heart's own private peace . . .

Dear Heaven, I give thanks to thee
For the things I did not know before,
For the wisdom of maturity,
For bread, and a roof, and for
    one thing more . . .

Thanks because I still can see
The bloom on the white magnolia tree!

HELEN DEUTSCH

I NEVER SAW A MOOR

I never saw a moor,
I never saw the sea;
Yet know I how the heather looks,
And what a wave must be.

I never spoke with God,
Nor visited in Heaven;
Yet certain am I of the spot
As if the chart were given.

EMILY DICKINSON

Parents — Children

CHARLIE and I reared our young during that period of terrorization of the parent—the 'Thirties and 'Forties, when everything we said could be used against us, or so the book told us. One slip of action, or one word, and our offspring could be marked for life. Every child who had the means had to have a bout with a child psychologist, his teeth straightened, and his vitamins toted up daily. And schedules: everything had to be meted out—play time, meal time, sleep time, reading time. From what I'm told, the situation has not changed very much since. The reign of terror continues, and parents are just plain scared stiff of their children.

Yet I do not notice that any master race has emerged from all the fear and fuss and books, of which there would surely be found to be a total of 10,000 if anyone were morbid enough to try to count them. But I do see a lot of bewildered people, young and old, trying to figure out what and who went wrong.

Perhaps we have been misguided into taking too much responsibility from our children, leaving them too little room for discovery. I know that we look with pity and concern on children who have to get up at the crack of dawn to help with chores on the farm, or go out to work before going to school. We are so pleased that we are able to free our children from those sterner realities. We feel that we have freed them for a fuller life. But what we've freed them from, it sometimes seems to me, is their sense of contribution to life, to family. Those who knew the harsher facts of life on the farm may have hated it, but subconsciously they were aware that they were contributing. I've had the feeling that I did not let my son Jim contribute enough as a member of our family and it has been a revelation to me as well as a source of great satisfaction to see him develop and grow in strength after he married and assumed the responsibility of raising a family.

I am always reading scoldings in the newspapers and the periodicals. And always the blame is placed on the parents. It's nearly always that parents must give more to their children, more love, more attention. But nowhere have I read that "You parents must *take* more from your children." What about asking the child to contribute something?

Isn't it possible that this lack of contribution, this lack of responsibility, is what makes so many of our young people today feel so lost? (Because goodness knows, they are.) Is this the reason perhaps why their efforts to express themselves are so inept and why they try to find their identity through funny haircuts, curious clothes, and worse.

I think in other ways, too, we do too much for our children. We try to make ourselves the buffer between them and reality. We create an artificial environment for them that must inevitably break down and leave them bewildered. I remember when Charlie was going into the service and I was going off on tour I was so full of fretting and anxiety about the reaction of the children that I turned to our family physician, who said, "Have you ever considered that these children will have to adjust to change at some time in their lives and if you don't begin to let them get used to change now, they're going to be pretty startled when they do have to make that adjustment when they are older?"

Charlie understood all this. When Charlie first saw our child, our Mary, he said all the proper things for a new father. He looked upon the poor little red thing and blurted, "She's more beautiful than the Brooklyn Bridge." On subsequent viewing when we three were alone, he stared at her long and solemnly and then said an odd thing, "We have given her birth and death and that's about all we can give her, really." I thought it morbid at the time because I was feeling all-powerful, as women do after childbirth. He was right, of course. It was life that would give her everything of consequence, life would shape her, not we. All we were good for was to make the introductions. We could introduce her to sights and sounds and sensations. How these reacted on her we must leave to her own private self. It is hard to accept this background position, and like most parents, we did not do it very well at all times. But we did at least understand our roles, and that is a step toward a passing performance.

In James M. Barrie's *Dear Brutus* there is a scene about poor Mr. Dearth's dream of himself and the daughter he would never have in reality. I played this scene when I was eighteen with the great William Gillette for more than a hundred nights, and I never got through it without an ache in my heart. And I still prefer Barrie's way of dealing with the truth about parents and children to that of any psychiatrist. As it is given here, the scene has been abridged.

MARGARET (*surveying him from another angle*). Now you are thinking about—about my being in love some day.

DEARTH (*with unnecessary warmth*). Rot!

MARGARET (*reassuringly*). I won't, you know; no, never. Oh, I have quite decided, so don't be afraid. (*Disordering his hair.*) Will you hate him at first, Daddy? Daddy, will you hate him? Will you hate him, Daddy?

DEARTH (*at work*). Whom?

MARGARET. Well, if there was?

DEARTH. If there was what, darling?

MARGARET. You know the kind of thing I mean, quite well. Would you hate him at first?

DEARTH. I hope not. I should want to strangle him, but I wouldn't hate him.

MARGARET. *I* would. That is to say, if I liked him.

DEARTH. If you liked him how could you hate him?

MARGARET. For daring!

DEARTH. Daring what?

MARGARET. You know. (*Sighing*) But of course I shall have no say in the matter. You will do it all. You do everything for me.

DEARTH (*with a groan*). I can't help it.

MARGARET. You will even write my love-letters, if I ever have any to write, which I won't.

DEARTH (*ashamed*). Surely to goodness, Margaret, I will leave you alone to do that!

MARGARET. Not you; you will try to, but you won't be able.

DEARTH (*in a hopeless attempt at self-defence*). I want you, you see, to do everything exquisitely. I do wish I could leave you to do things a little more for yourself.

I suppose it's owing to my having had to be father and mother both. I knew nothing practically about the bringing up of children, and of course I couldn't trust you to a nurse.

MARGARET. Dad, if I ever should marry—not that I will, but if I should—at the marriage ceremony will you let me be the one who says 'I do'?

DEARTH. I suppose I deserve this.

MARGARET (*coaxingly*). You think I'm pretty, don't you, Dad, whatever other people say?

DEARTH. Not so bad.

MARGARET. I *know* I have nice ears.

DEARTH. They are all right now, but I had to work on them for months.

MARGARET. You don't mean to say that you did my *ears*?

DEARTH. Rather!

MARGARET (*grown humble*). My dimple is my own.

DEARTH. I am glad you think so. I wore out the point of my little finger over that dimple.

MARGARET. Even my dimple! Have I anything that is really mine? A bit of my nose or anything?

DEARTH. When you were a babe you had a laugh that was all your own.

MARGARET. Haven't I got it now?

DEARTH. It's gone. (*He looks ruefully at her.*) I'll tell you how it went. We were fishing in a stream—that is to say, I was wading and you were sitting on my shoulders holding the rod. We didn't catch anything. Somehow or another—I can't think how I did it—you irritated me, and I answered you sharply.

MARGARET (*gasping*). I can't believe that.

DEARTH. Yes, it sounds extraordinary, but I did. It gave you a shock, and, for the moment, the world no longer seemed a safe place to you; your faith in me had always made it safe till then. You were suddenly not even sure of your bread and butter, and a frightened tear came to your eyes. I was in a nice state about it, I can tell you. (*He is in a nice state about it still.*)

MARGARET. Silly! (*Bewildered*) But what has that to do with my laugh, Daddy?

DEARTH. The laugh that children are born with lasts just so long as they have perfect faith. To think that it was I who robbed you of yours!

MARGARET. Don't, dear. I am sure the laugh just went off with the tear to comfort it, and they have been playing about that stream ever since. They have quite forgotten us, so why should we remember them. Cheeky little beasts! Shall I tell you my farthest-back recollection? (*In some awe*) I remember the first time I saw the stars. I had never seen night, and then I saw it and the stars together. Crack-in-my-eye Tommy, it isn't every one who can boast of such a lovely, lovely recollection for their earliest, is it?

DEARTH. I was determined your earliest should be a good one.

MARGARET (*blankly*). Do you mean to say you planned it?

DEARTH. Rather! Most people's earliest recollection is of some trivial thing; how they cut their finger, or lost a piece of string. I was resolved my Margaret's should be something bigger. I was poor, but I could give her the stars.

MARGARET (*clutching him round the legs*). Oh, how you love me.

DEARTH. Yes, I do, rather.

When Mary was one year old F. Scott Fitzgerald came up to visit us in Nyack, and Charlie, proud father that he was, immediately insisted on taking Scott into the nursery. He was anxious for Mary to perform for Scott, having already boasted to his friend that his name was the first she'd learned. Mary looked Scott squarely in his blue eyes and said, "Papa, papa." The fact is that that is what Mary called every one of Charlie's friends. And he became so infuriated he was figuratively kicking the furniture and saying, "She's undoing me, and at a year old, too." Scott wrote this little poem for Mary to commemorate his visit:

> "Oh papa—
> My papa—
> Say papa—"
> So!

> "Is papa
> Your papa
> My papa?"
> No!

> So spoke you—
> Why joke you?
> Just for today

> One word is
> (like birdie's)
> Plenty to say.

When Mary was three Noel Coward wrote the following in her Birthday Book.

ON MARY MacARTHUR'S THIRD BIRTHDAY

> With pleasure Miss MacArthur dear
> I venture to inscribe
> The following polite, sincere

And gentle diatribe.
To one fact pray be reconciled,
　　Admit no "ifs" nor "buts,"
Your mother is an actress, child,
　　And consequently "nuts"!
There's one more fact that you must list
　　And face, for good or bad,
Your father is a dramatist
　　And consequently mad.
Whichever way your fortune bends
　　And circumstances change,
Your mother's and your father's friends
　　Are certain to be strange.
In all this odd, eccentric clan
　　Just one exception shines—
The *talented* and *witty* man
　　Who wrote these charming lines!

NOEL COWARD

And Scott wrote another when Mary was eight.

FOR MARY'S EIGHTH BIRTHDAY

What shall I do with this bundle of stuff,
Mass of ingredients, handful of grist,
Tenderest evidence, thumbprint of lust,
Kindly advise me, O Psychologist.
She shall have music—we pray for the kiss
Of the gods on her forehead, her necking of fate.
How in the hell shall we guide her to this
"—Just name her Mary and age her till eight."
What of the books? Do we feed her on bread
Of the dead, that was left in their tombs long ago?
Or should all the fervor and freshness be wed

To next year's inventions? Can anyone know?
How shall we give her that *Je ne sais quoi*—
Portions of mama that seem to be right,
Salted with dashes of questionable pa?
"—Age her till eight and then save me a bite."
How can I pay back this heavenly loan?
Answer my question and name your own fee;
Plan me a mixture of Eve and St. Joan,
"—Put her in pigtails and give her to me."

F. SCOTT FITZGERALD

I always have felt, indeed, I am almost sure, that as Scott
and Noel did, so Swinburne wrote the following lovely poem
for a friend's child.

A CHILD'S LAUGHTER

All the bells of heaven may ring,
All the birds of heaven may sing,
All the wells on earth may spring,
All the winds on earth may bring
    All sweet sounds together;
Sweeter far than all things heard,
Hand of harper, tone of bird,
Sound of woods at sundawn stirred,
Welling water's winsome word,
    Wind in warm wan weather,

One thing yet there is, that none
Hearing ere its chime be done
Knows not well the sweetest one
Heard of man beneath the sun,
    Hoped in heaven hereafter;
Soft and strong and loud and light,

Very sound of very light
Heard from morning's rosiest height,
When the soul of all delight
    Fills a child's clear laughter.

Golden bells of welcome rolled
Never forth such notes, nor told
Hours so blithe in tone so bold,
As the radiant mouth of gold
    Here that rings forth heaven.
If the golden-crested wren
Were a nightingale—why, then,
Something seen and heard of men
Might be half as sweet as when
    Laughs a child of seven.

ALGERNON CHARLES SWINBURNE

Charlie gave me this to read shortly after our daughter was born. He had found it in W. H. Prescott's *History of the Conquest of Mexico.*

ADVICE OF AN AZTEC MOTHER
TO HER DAUGHTER

My beloved daughter, very dear little dove, you have already heard and attended to the words which your father has told you. They are precious words, and such as are rarely spoken or listened to, and which have proceeded from the bowels and heart, in which they were treasured up; and your beloved father well knows that you are his daughter, begotten of him, are his blood, and his flesh; and God our Lord knows that it is so. Although you are a woman, and are *the image of your father*, what more can I say to you than has already

been said? What more can you hear than what you have
heard from your lord and father? who has fully told you
what it is becoming for you to do and to avoid, nor is
there any thing remaining which concerns you, that he
has not touched upon. Nevertheless, that I may do towards you my whole duty, I will say to you some few
words.—The first thing that I earnestly charge upon you
is, that you observe and do not forget what your father
has now told you, since it is all very precious; and persons of his condition rarely publish such things; for they
are the words which belong to the noble and wise,—
valuable as rich jewels. See, then, that you take them
and lay them up in your heart, and write them in your
bowels. If God gives you life, with these same words
will you teach your sons and daughters, if God shall
give you them.—The second thing that I desire to say
to you is, that I love you much, that you are my dear
daughter. Remember that nine months I bore you in
my womb, that you were born and brought up in my
arms. I placed you in your cradle, and in my lap, and
with my milk I nursed you. This I tell you, in order that
you may know that I and your father are the source of
your being; it is we who now instruct you. See that you
receive our words, and treasure them in your breast.—
Take care that your garments are such as are decent and
proper; and observe that you do not adorn yourself with
much finery, since this is a mark of vanity and of folly.
As little becoming is it, that your dress should be very
mean, dirty, or ragged; since rags are a mark of the low,
and of those who are held in contempt. Let your clothes
be becoming and neat, that you may neither appear
fantastic nor mean. When you speak, do not hurry your
words from uneasiness, but speak deliberately and
calmly. Do not raise your voice very high, nor speak
very low, but in a moderate tone. Neither mince, when
you speak, nor when you salute, nor speak through your

nose; but let your words be proper, of a good sound, and your voice gentle. Do not be nice in the choice of your words. In walking, my daughter, see that you behave becomingly, neither going with haste, nor too slowly; since it is an evidence of being puffed up, to walk too slowly, and walking hastily causes a vicious habit of restlessness and instability. Therefore neither walk very fast, nor very slow; yet, when it shall be necessary to go with haste, do so,—in this use your discretion. And when you may be obliged to jump over a pool of water, do it with decency, that you may neither appear clumsy nor light. When you are in the street, do not carry your head much inclined, or your body bent; nor as little go with your head very much raised; since it is a mark of ill breeding; walk erect, and with your head slightly inclined. Do not have your mouth covered, or your face, from shame, nor go looking like a near-sighted person, nor, on your way, make fantastic movements with your feet. Walk through the street quietly, and with propriety. Another thing that you must attend to, my daughter, is, that, when you are in the street, you do not go looking hither and thither, nor turning your head to look at this and that; walk neither looking at the skies, nor on the ground. Do not look upon those whom you meet with the eyes of an offended person, nor have the appearance of being uneasy; but of one who looks upon all with a serene countenance; doing this, you will give no one occasion of being offended with you. Show a becoming countenance; that you may neither appear morose, nor, on the other hand, too complaisant. See, my daughter, that you give yourself no concern about the words you may hear, in going through the street, nor pay any regard to them, let those who come and go say what they will. Take care that you neither answer nor speak, but act as if you neither heard nor understood them; since, doing in this manner, no one will be

able to say with truth that you have said any thing
amiss. See, likewise, my daughter, that you never paint
your face, or stain it or your lips with colors, in order to
appear well; since this is a mark of vile and unchaste
women. Paints and coloring are things which bad
women use,—the immodest, who have lost all shame and
even sense, who are like fools and drunkards, and are
called *rameras* [prostitutes]. But, that your husband
may not dislike you, adorn yourself, wash yourself, and
cleanse your clothes; and let this be done with modera-
tion; since, if every day you wash yourself and your
clothes, it will be said of you, that you are overnice,—too
delicate; they will call you *tapepetzon tinemaxoch*.—My
daughter, this is the course you are to take; since in this
manner the ancestors from whom you spring brought us
up. Those noble and venerable dames, your grand-
mothers, told us not so many things as I have told you,—
they said but few words, and spoke thus: "Listen, my
daughters; in this world, it is necessary to live with
much prudence and circumspection. Hear this allegory,
which I shall now tell you, and preserve it, and take
from it a warning and example for living aright. Here,
in this world, we travel by a very narrow, steep, and
dangerous road, which is as a lofty mountain ridge, on
whose top passes a narrow path; on either side is a great
gulf without bottom, and, if you deviate from the path,
you will fall into it. There is need, therefore, of much
discretion in pursuing the road." My tenderly loved
daughter, my little dove, keep this illustration in your
heart, and see that you do not forget it,—it will be to
you as a lamp and a beacon, so long as you shall live in
this world.—Only one thing remains to be said, and I
have done. If God shall give you life, if you shall continue some years upon the earth, see that you guard
yourself carefully, that no stain come upon you; should
you forfeit your chastity, and afterwards be asked in

marriage and should marry any one, you will never be fortunate, nor have true love,—he will always remember that you were not a virgin, and this will be the cause of great affliction and distress; you will never be at peace, for your husband will always be suspicious of you. O, my dearly beloved daughter, if you shall live upon the earth, see that not more than one man approaches you; and observe what I now shall tell you, as a strict command. When it shall please God that you receive a husband, and you are placed under his authority, be free from arrogance, see that you do not neglect him, nor allow your heart to be in opposition to him. Be not disrespectful to him. Beware, that, in no time or place, you commit the treason against him called adultery. See that you give no favor to another; since this, my dear and much loved daughter, is to fall into a pit without bottom, from which there will be no escape. According to the custom of the world, if it shall be known, for this crime they will kill you, they will throw you into the street, for an example to all the people, where your head will be crushed and dragged upon the ground. Of these says a proverb: "You will be stoned and dragged upon the earth, and others will take warning at your death." From this will arise a stain and dishonor upon our ancestors, the nobles and senators from whom we are descended. You will tarnish their illustrious fame, and their glory, by the filthiness and impurity of your sin. You will, likewise, lose your reputation, your nobility, and honor of birth; your name will be forgotten and abhorred. Of you will it be said, that you were buried in the dust of your sins. And remember, my daughter, that, though no man shall see you, nor your husband ever know what happens, *God, who is in every place, sees you*, will be angry with you, and will also excite the indignation of the people against you, and will be avenged upon you as he shall see fit. By his command,

you shall either be maimed, or struck blind, or your
body will wither, or you will come to extreme poverty,
for daring to injure your husband. Or, perhaps, he will
give you to death, and put you under his feet, sending
you to the place of torment. Our Lord is compassionate;
but, if you commit treason against your husband, God,
who is in every place, shall take vengeance on your sin,
and will permit you to have neither contentment, nor
repose, nor a peaceful life; and he will excite your husband to be always unkind towards you, and always to
speak to you with anger. My dear daughter, whom I
tenderly love, see that you live in the world in peace,
tranquillity, and contentment, all the days that you shall
live. See that you disgrace not yourself, that you stain
not your honor, nor pollute the lustre and fame of your
ancestors. See that you honor me and your father, and
reflect glory on us by your good life. May God prosper
you, my first-born, and may you come to God, who is in
every place.

AUTOBIOGRAPHY

In my childhood trees were green
And there was plenty to be seen.

Come back early or never come.

My father made the walls resound,
He wore his collar the wrong way round.

Come back early or never come.

My mother wore a yellow dress;
Gently, gently, gentleness.

Come back early or never come.

When I was five the black dreams came;
Nothing after was quite the same.

Come back early or never come.

The dark was talking to the dead
The lamp was dark beside my bed.

Come back early or never come.

When I woke they did not care;
Nobody, nobody was there.

Come back early or never come.

When my silent terror cried,
Nobody, nobody replied.

Come back early or never come.

I got up; the chilly sun
Saw me walk away alone.

Come back early or never come.

LOUIS MACNEICE

From THE PROPHET

... Your children are not your children.
They are the sons and daughters of Life's
    longing for itself.
They come through you but not from you,
And though they are with you yet they
    belong not to you.
You may give them your love but not your
    thoughts,

For they have their own thoughts.
You may house their bodies but not their
    souls,
For their souls dwell in the house of
    tomorrow, which you cannot visit, not
    even in your dreams.
You may strive to be like them, but seek
    not to make them like you.
For life goes not backward nor tarries
    with yesterday.

KAHLIL GIBRAN

From ODE: INTIMATIONS OF IMMORTALITY

Our birth is but a sleep and a forgetting:
The Soul that rises with us, our life's Star,
    Hath had elsewhere its setting,
    And cometh from afar:
    Not in entire forgetfulness,
    And not in utter nakedness,
But trailing clouds of glory do we come
    From God, who is our home:
Heaven lies about us in our infancy!
Shades of the prison-house begin to close
    Upon the growing Boy,
But he beholds the light, and whence it flows,
    He sees it in his joy;
The Youth, who daily farther from the East
    Must travel, still is Nature's Priest,
    And by the vision spendid
    Is on his way attended;
At length the Man perceives it die away,
And fade into the light of common day.

WILLIAM WORDSWORTH

THERE WAS A CHILD WENT FORTH

There was child went forth every day,
And the first object he look'd upon, that object he
became,
And that object became part of him for the day or a
certain part of the day,
Or for many years or stretching cycles of years.
The early lilacs became part of this child,
And grass and white and red morning-glories, and white
and red clover, and the song of the phœbe-bird,
And the Third-month lambs and the sow's pink-faint
litter, and the mare's foal and the cow's calf,
And the noisy brood of the barnyard or by the mire of
the pond-side,
And the fish suspending themselves so curiously below
there, and the beautiful curious liquid,
And the water-plants with their graceful flat heads, all
became part of him.

The field-sprouts of Fourth-month and Fifth-month became part of him,
Winter-grain sprouts and those of the light-yellow corn,
and the esculent roots of the garden,
And the apple-trees cover'd with blossoms and the fruit
afterward, and wood-berries, and the commonest
weeds by the road,
And the old drunkard staggering home from the out-
house of the tavern whence he had lately risen,
And the schoolmistress that pass'd on her way to the
school,
And the friendly boys that pass'd and the quarrelsome
boys,
And the tidy and fresh-cheek'd girls, and the barefoot
negro boy and girl,

And all the changes of city and country wherever he
went.

His own parents, he that had father'd him and she that
had conceiv'd him in her womb and birth'd him,
They gave this child more of themselves than that,
They gave him afterward every day, they became part
of him.

The mother at home quietly placing the dishes on the
supper-table,
The mother with mild words, clean her cap and gown, a
wholesome odor falling off her person and clothes
as she walks by,
The father, strong, self-sufficient, manly, mean, anger'd,
unjust,
The blow, the quick loud word, the tight bargain, the
crafty lure,
The family usages, the language, the company, the
furniture, the yearning and swelling heart,
Affection that will not be gainsay'd, the sense of what is
real, the thought if after all it should prove unreal,
The doubts of day-time and the doubts of night-time,
the curious whether and how,
Whether that which appears so is so, or is it all flashes
and specks?
Men and women crowding fast in the streets, if they are
not flashes and specks what are they?
The streets themselves and the façades of houses, and
goods in the windows,
Vehicles, teams, the heavy-plank'd wharves, the huge
crossing at the ferries,
The village on the highland seen from afar at sunset,
the river between,
Shadows, aureola and mist, the light falling on roofs and
gables of white or brown two miles off,

The schooner near by sleepily dropping down the tide,
  the little boat slack-tow'd astern,
The hurrying tumbling waves, quick-broken crests,
  slapping,
The strata of color'd clouds, the long bar of maroon-tint
  away solitary by itself, the spread of purity it lies
  motionless in,
The horizon's edge, the flying sea-crow, the fragrance of
  salt marsh and shore mud,
These became part of that child who went forth every
  day, and who now goes, and will always go forth
  every day.

                                        WALT WHITMAN

THE CHILDREN'S HOUR

Between the dark and the daylight,
  When the night is beginning to lower,
Comes a pause in the day's occupations,
  That is known as the Children's Hour.

I hear in the chamber above me
  The patter of little feet,
The sound of a door that is opened,
  And voices soft and sweet.

From my study I see in the lamplight,
  Descending the broad hall stair,
Grave Alice, and laughing Allegra,
  And Edith with golden hair.

A whisper, and then a silence:
  Yet I know by their merry eyes
They are plotting and planning together
  To take me by surprise.

A sudden rush from the stairway,
  A sudden raid from the hall!
By three doors left unguarded
  They enter my castle wall!

They climb up into my turret
  O'er the arms and back of my chair;
If I try to escape, they surround me;
  They seem to be everywhere.

They almost devour me with kisses,
  Their arms about me entwine,
Till I think of the Bishop of Bingen
  In his Mouse-Tower on the Rhine!

Do you think, O blue-eyed banditti,
  Because you have scaled the wall,
Such an old mustache as I am
  Is not a match for you all!

I have you fast in my fortress,
  And will not let you depart,
But put you down into the dungeon
  In the round-tower of my heart.

And there will I keep you forever,
  Yes, forever and a day,
Till the walls shall crumble to ruin,
And moulder in dust away.

HENRY WADSWORTH LONGFELLOW

From AMERICAN CHILD

She is a miracle like daily light,
As warm, as moving as that luminous air.

Let her eyes never lose the daily sight
Of the sun's great golden hand on face and hair.
Let all her talk be water from a sweet well,
Tasting of sandy earth, the deep drowned stone.
One sudden day, with strangers, we will tell:
Here is a girl. But look—a woman grown.

Let her live, then, so she may understand
That final, negative and human crime:
Not to learn, in the false fear of too much,
The secret and intolerable touch
From passionate mind and intellectual hand
Of love that knows times when it can know no time.

PAUL ENGLE

GOOD AND BAD CHILDREN

Children, you are very little,
And your bones are very brittle;
If you would grow great and stately,
You must try to walk sedately.

You must still be bright and quiet,
And content with simple diet;
And remain, through all bewild'ring,
Innocent and honest children.

Happy hearts and happy faces,
Happy play in grassy places—
That was how, in ancient ages,
Children grew to kings and sages.

But the unkind and the unruly,
And the sort who eat unduly,
They must never hope for glory—
Theirs is quite a different story!

Cruel children, crying babies,
All grow up as geese and gabies,
Hated, as their age increases,
By their nephews and their nieces.

ROBERT LOUIS STEVENSON

PATERFAMILIAS

Of all the saints who have won their charter—
Holy man, hero, hermit, martyr,
Mystic, missioner, sage, or wit—
Saint Thomas More is my favorite.
For he loved these bounties with might and main:
God and his house and his little wife, Jane,
And four fair children his heart throve on,
Margaret, Elizabeth, Cecily, and John.

That More was a good man everybody knows.
He sang good verses and he wrote good prose,
Enjoyed a good caper and liked a good meal
And made a good Master of the Privy Seal.
A friend to Erasmus, Lily's friend,
He lived a good life and he had a good end
And left good counsel for them to con,
Margaret, Elizabeth, Cecily, and John.

Some saints are alien, hard to love,
Wild as an eagle, strange as a dove,
Too near to heaven for the mind to scan.
But Thomas More was a family man,
A husband, a courtier, a doer and a hoper
(Admired of his son-in-law, Mr. Roper),
Who punned in Latin like a Cambridge don
With Margaret, Elizabeth, Cecily, and John.

It was less old Henry than Anne Boleyn
Hailed him to the Tower and locked him in.
But even in the Tower he saw things brightly.
He spoke to his jailers most politely,
And while the sorrowers turned their backs
He rallied the headsman who held the ax,
Then blessed, with the blessing of Thomas More,
God and his garden and his children four.

And I fear they missed him when he was gone—
Margaret, Elizabeth, Cecily, and John.

PHYLLIS MC GINLEY

From MY LITTLE BOY

We have beer-soup and Aunt Anna to dinner. Now beer-soup is a nasty dish and Aunt Anna is not very nice either.

She has yellow teeth and a little hump and very severe eyes, which are not even both equally severe. She is nearly always scolding us and, when she sees a chance, she pinches us.

The worst of all, however, is that she is constantly setting us a good example, which can easily end by gradually and inevitably driving us to embrace wickedness.

Aunt Anna does not like beer-soup any more than we do. But of course she eats it with a voluptuous expression on her face and looks angrily at my little boy, who does not even make an attempt to behave nicely:

"Why doesn't the little boy eat his delicious beer-soup?" she asks.

A scornful silence.

"Such delicious beer-soup! I know a poor, wretched boy who would be awfully glad to have such delicious beer-soup."

My little boy looks with great interest at Auntie, who is swallowing her soup with eyes full of ecstatic bliss:

"Where is he?" he asks.

Aunt Anna pretends not to hear.

"Where is the poor boy?" he asks again.

"Yes, where is he?" I ask. "What's his name?"

Aunt Anna gives me a furious glance.

"What's his name, Aunt Anna?" asks my little boy. "Where does he live? He can have my beer-soup with pleasure."

"Mine too," I say, resolutely, and I push my plate from me.

My little boy never takes his great eyes off Aunt Anna's face. Meanwhile, she has recovered herself:

"There are many poor boys who would thank God if they could get such delicious beer-soup," she says. "Very many. Everywhere."

"Yes, but tell us of one, Auntie," I say.

My little boy has slipped down from his chair. He stands with his chin just above the table and both his hands round his plate, ready to march off with the beer-soup to the poor boy, if only he can get his address.

But Aunt Anna does not allow herself to be played with:

"Heaps of poor boys," she says again. "Hun-dreds! And therefore another little boy, whom I will not name, but who is in this room, ought to be ashamed that he is not thankful for his beer-soup."

My little boy stares at Aunt Anna like the bird fascinated by the snake.

"Such delicious beer-soup!" she says. "I must really ask for another little helping."

Aunt Anna revels in her martyrdom. My little boy stands speechless, with open mouth and round eyes.

I push my chair back and say, with genuine exasperation:

"Now, look here, Aunt Anna, this is really too bad! Here we are, with a whole lot of beer-soup, which we don't care about in the least and which we would be very glad to get rid of, if we only knew some one who would have it. You are the only one that knows of anybody. You know a poor boy who would dance for joy if he got some beer-soup. You know hundreds. But you won't tell us their names or where they live."

"Why, what do you mean?"

"And you yourself sit quite calmly eating two whole helpings, though you know quite well that you're going to have an omelette to follow. That's really very naughty of you, Aunt Anna."

Aunt Anna chokes with annoyance. My little boy locks his teeth with a snap and looks with every mark of disgust at that wicked old woman.

And I turn with calm earnestness to his mother and say:

"After this, it would be most improper for us ever to have beer-soup here again. We don't care for it and there are hundreds of little boys who love it. If it must be made, then Aunt Anna must come every Saturday and fetch it. She knows where the boys live."

The omelette is eaten in silence, after which Aunt Anna shakes the dust from her shoes. She won't have any coffee to-day.

While she is standing in the hall and putting on her endless wraps, a last doubt arises in my little boy's soul. He opens his green eyes wide before her face and whispers:

"Aunt Anna where do the boys live?"

Aunt Anna pinches him and is shocked and goes off, having suffered a greater defeat than she can ever repair.

*   *   *

Here ends this book about my little boy.
What more can there be to tell?

He is no longer mine. I have handed him over to society. Hr. Petersen, candidate in letters, Hr. Nielsen, student of theology, and Fröken Hansen, certificated teacher, will now set their distinguished example before him for five hours daily. He will form himself in their likeness. Their spirit hovers over him at school: he brings it home with him, it overshadows him when he is learning the lessons which they zealously mete out to him.

I don't know these people. But I pay them.

I, who have had a hard fight to keep my thoughts free and my limbs unrestrained and who have not retired from the fight without deep wounds of which I am reminded when the weather changes, I have, of my own free will, brought him to the institution for maiming human beings. I, who at times have soared to peaks that were my own, because the other birds dared not follow me, have myself brought him to the place where wings are clipped for flying respectably, with the flock.

"There was nothing else to be done," says the mother of my little boy.

"Really?" I reply, bitterly. "Was there nothing else to be done? But suppose that I had put by some money, so that I could have saved Messrs. Petersen and Nielsen and Fröken Hansen their trouble and employed my day in myself opening out lands for that little traveller whom I myself have brought into the land? Suppose that I had looked round the world for people with small boys who think as I do and that we had taken upon us to bring up these young animals so that they kept sight of horns and tails and fairy-tales?"

"Yes," she says.

"Small boys have a bad time of it, you know."

"They had a worse time of it in the old days."

"That is a poor comfort. And it can become worse again. The world is full of parents and teachers who shake their foolish heads and turn up their old eyes and cross their flat chests with horror at the depravity of youth: children are so disobedient, so naughty, so self-willed and talk so disrespectfully to their elders! . . . And what do we do, we who know better?"

"We do what we can."

But I walk about the room, more and more indignant and ashamed of the pitiful part which I am playing:

"Do you remember, a little while ago, he came to me and said that he longed so for the country and asked if we couldn't go there for a little? There were horses and cows and green fields to be read in his eyes. Well, I couldn't leave my work. And I couldn't afford it. So I treated him to a shabby and high-class sermon about the tailor to whom I owed money. Don't you understand that I let my little boy do *my* work, that I let him pay *my* debt? . . ." I bend down over her and say earnestly, "You must know; do please tell me—God help me, I do not know—if I ought not rather to have paid my debt to the boy and cheated the other?"

"You know quite well," she says.

She says it in such a way and looks at me with two such sensible eyes and is so strong and so true that I suddenly think things look quite well for our little boy; and I become restful and cheerful like herself:

"Let Petersen and Nielsen and Hansen look out!" I say. "My little boy, for what I care, may take from them all the English and geography and history that he can. But they shall throw no dust in his eyes. I shall keep him awake and we shall have great fun and find them out."

"And I shall help him with his English and geography and history," says she.

CARL EWALD

Solitude

THERE is another place besides my Nyack garden where I find the gift of joy provided by solitude. And that is in my *Casa Serena*—my serene house, as it was named, —in Cuernavaca, an hour's drive from Mexico City on the road to Acapulco.

I found Cuernavaca many years ago through my brother-in-law, Alfred MacArthur and his wife Mary, who had bought a house there, next to one owned by Dwight Morrow when he was our ambassador to Mexico. I had become extremely fond of this little city in the State of Morelos. Nestling in the mountains at a height of about 5,000 feet, it was called by the Aztecs, before the Conquest, Cuauhna-huac, which means "Near Wooded Mountains." And so some years ago when I felt I needed a retreat from the pressures of my life, I bought a little house there on the Calle Victoria. For several months out of each year I am able to find comfort and seclusion within its walls. The climate is even in this city of eternal spring. But there is no end to the surprises

I find here. I never tire of walking and exploring its crooked little streets with their gaily colored houses. Flowering trees, tropical fruits, palms, and orchids grow in profusion. And everywhere there are the flaming bougainvillea.

Although the garden of my *Casa Serena* is small and there aren't my beloved roses, or the crocuses, or jonquils, or any dogwood, which was Charlie's favorite and which I came to treasure because I gloried in the joy it gave him, there are other beauties. Outside my bedroom window there is an excitingly shaped wild plum tree. And there is an exquisite orchid tree—which the humming birds love. There is a banana tree. And there are the surrounding mountains, especially those two breathtaking snowcapped volcanoes, Ixtaci-huatl (the White, or Sleeping, Lady) and Popocatepetl (Smoking Mountain) which rise to a height of 17,000 feet. They are remote and full of mystery and I thank goodness that my house faces them. They say in Cuernavaca that this is the only city in the world where you look east for the sunset. Because on these two mountains—on the white peak of Popo and the long, white shimmering body of the Lady— you see the reflection of the sun when it sets, and it is a tonic for the spirit. These two mountains spell for me eternal peace and the age of Mexico. To many descendants of the Aztecs they represent a force greater than mere mountains, and in pre-Conquest days they were worshiped as deities. One of the most romantic of the legends associated with these moun-tains says that Ixtacihuatl was the daughter of a king and that she had had a love affair with a young warrior, Popo-catepetl. When their love was discovered, he fled and left her to face the consequences alone. He was killed in war and she eventually died of a broken heart. So he was sentenced by the gods to stand guard over her as she slept her eternal sleep. But, because they were lovers and had loved so well, the gods relented to the extent that they gave the pair one month a year so that they might disappear and go to heaven, from which they have otherwise been barred. And that one month, from about early October until about the middle of November, you cannot see them at all. There is just no trace of them even on clear days when there is no mist.

Most of us are in constant search of a Shangri-la, a Bali Hai, a Walden. I find mine in Cuernavaca. Just before my last visit, a devoted friend said to me, "I really don't understand how you can go off to Mexico and stay away from all the people who love you. How can you want to be alone there?" And I said, "You know, I think I'm a little bit too much beloved. Nobody gives a good darn about me in Mexico. They don't know I'm famous. They don't know anything about me and I can be left blissfully alone there."

What my friend could not understand is that I am not lonely in Cuernavaca. Surely I have friends there. But that's not the point. There is a difference between solitude and loneliness. Loneliness is something within us, whereas solitude is a way of existence. You can be lonely anywhere; you can be lonely in a crowd. But the solitude I seek and find in Cuernavaca is quite a different thing. When you do not have a lonely heart, or a lonely spirit, you are able to be beguiled, in solitude, by all kinds of things—a bird that flashes by, or the shape of a leaf. This is an experience that is just as rewarding, perhaps, as a companion who says something that is pleasing to you. You make your company and make your companionship out of all the things around you.

In the very rare and treasured times when I have my solitude, my greatest reward is that I am able to make some infinitesimally small progress toward acquaintance with myself, something you cannot do unless you can be alone and therefore free.

There are other fruits of solitude. It enables me to avail myself a little bit more of the pleasures so many of us look forward to in life, like being able to read and concentrate on what we're reading, something I find very difficult to do when I'm surrounded by loving friends and the intrusion of well-meaning people. I find that when I am home in Nyack I read a whole page of a book, a book that I've been hungering for, and I have to go back and read it again because I virtually don't know what I've read. My mind has been shooting off in other directions—to what I must do tomorrow, to what I forgot to do today, or to having to phone somebody about some quite unimportant matter. But when I get to hide in my garden, or go on a long walk, or settle down briefly in Cuernavaca, my mind relaxes and it is receptive to the things I am so anxious to enjoy.

We live in a very tense society. We are pulled apart as if by centrifugal force and we all need to learn how to pull ourselves together. Pull ourselves together—we all use that phrase, but too many of us aren't trained for that job of literally pulling ourselves together so that we can function as full human beings. I think that at least part of the answer lies in solitude.

OF FRIENDSHIP

But little do men perceive what solitude is, and how far it extendeth. For a crowd is not company; and faces are but a gallery of pictures; and talk but a tinkling cymbal, where there is no love.

SIR FRANCIS BACON

SOLITUDE

This is a delicious evening, when the whole body is one sense, and imbibes delight through every pore. I go and come with a strange liberty in Nature, a part of herself. As I walk along the stony shore of the pond in my shirt-sleeves, though it is cool as well as cloudy and windy, and I see nothing special to attract me, all the elements are unusually congenial to me. The bullfrogs trump to usher in the night, and the note of the whip-poor-will is borne on the rippling wind from over the water. Sympathy with the fluttering alder and poplar leaves almost takes away my breath; yet, like the lake, my serenity is rippled but not ruffled. These small waves raised by the evening wind are as remote from storm as the smooth reflecting surface. Though it is now dark, the wind still blows and roars in the wood, the waves still dash, and some creatures lull the rest with their notes. The repose is never complete. The wildest animals do not repose, but seek their prey now; the fox, and skunk, and rabbit, now roam the fields and woods without fear. They are Nature's watchmen,—links which connect the days of animated life.

When I return to my house I find that visitors have been there and left their cards, either a bunch of flowers, or a wreath of evergreen, or a name in pencil on a yellow walnut leaf or a chip. They who come rarely to the woods take some little piece of the forest into their hands to play with by the way, which they leave, either intentionally or accidentally. One has peeled a willow wand, woven it into a ring, and dropped it on my table. I could always tell if visitors had called in my absence, either by the bended twigs or grass, or the print of their shoes, and generally of what sex or age or quality they were by some slight trace left, as a flower dropped, or a bunch of grass plucked and thrown away, even as far off as the railroad, half a mile distant, or by the lingering odor of a cigar or pipe. Nay, I was frequently notified of the passage of a traveller along the highway sixty rods off by the scent of his pipe.

There is commonly sufficient space about us. Our horizon is never quite at our elbows. The thick woods is not just at our door, nor the pond, but somewhat is always clearing, familiar and worn by us, appropriated and fenced in some way, and reclaimed from Nature. For what reason have I this vast range and circuit, some square miles of unfrequented forest, for my privacy, abandoned to me by men? My nearest neighbor is a mile distant, and no house is visible from any place but the hill-tops within half a mile of my own. I have my horizon bounded by woods all to myself; a distant view of the railroad where it touches the pond on the one hand, and of the fence which skirts the woodland road on the other. But for the most part it is as solitary where I live as on the prairies. It is as much Asia or Africa as New England. I have, as it were, my own sun and moon and stars, and a little world all to myself. At night there was never a traveller passed my house, or knocked at my door, more than if I were the first or last man; unless it were in the spring, when at long intervals some came from the village to fish for pouts,—they plainly fished much more in the Walden Pond of their own natures, and baited their hooks with darkness,—but they soon retreated, usually with light baskets, and left "the world to darkness and to me," and the black kernel of the night was never profaned by any human neighborhood. I believe that men are generally still a little afraid of the dark, though the witches are all hung, and Christianity and candles have been introduced.

Yet I experienced sometimes that the most sweet and tender, the most innocent and encouraging society may

be found in any natural object, even for the poor misanthrope and most melancholy man. There can be no very
black melancholy to him who lives in the midst of Nature
and has his senses still. There was never yet such a storm
but it was Aeolian music to a healthy and innocent ear.
Nothing can rightly compel a simple and brave man to
a vulgar sadness. While I enjoy the friendship of the
seasons I trust that nothing can make life a burden to
me. The gentle rain which waters my beans and keeps
me in the house today is not drear and melancholy, but
good for me too. Though it prevents my hoeing them,
it is of far more worth than my hoeing. If it should continue so long as to cause the seeds to rot in the ground
and destroy the potatoes in the low lands, it would still
be good for the grass on the uplands, and, being good
for the grass, it would be good for me. Sometimes, when
I compare myself with other men, it seems as if I were
more favored by the gods than they, beyond any deserts
that I am conscious of; as if I had a warrant and surety
at their hands which my fellows have not, and were
especially guided and guarded. I do not flatter myself,
but if it be possible they flatter me. I have never felt
lonesome, or in the least oppressed by a sense of solitude, but once, and that was a few weeks after I came
to the woods, when, for an hour, I doubted if the near
neighborhood of man was not essential to a serene and
healthy life. To be alone was something unpleasant. But
I was at the same time conscious of a slight insanity
in my mood, and seemed to foresee my recovery. In the
midst of a gentle rain while these thoughts prevailed,
I was suddenly sensible of such sweet and beneficent
society in Nature, in the very pattering of the drops, and
in every sound and sight around my house, an infinite
and unaccountable friendliness all at once like an atmosphere sustaining me, as made the fancied advantages
of human neighborhood insignificant, and I have never

thought of them since. Every little pine needle expanded and swelled with sympathy and befriended me. I was so distinctly made aware of the presence of something kindred to me, even in scenes which we are accustomed to call wild and dreary, and also that the nearest of blood to me and humanest was not a person nor a villager, that I thought no place could ever be strange to me again.—

"Mourning untimely consumes the sad;
Few are their days in the land of the living,
Beautiful daughter of Toscar."

Some of my pleasantest hours were during the long rainstorms in the spring or fall, which confined me to the house for the afternoon as well as the forenoon, soothed by their ceaseless roar and pelting; when an early twilight ushered in a long evening in which many thoughts had time to take root and unfold themselves. In those driving northeast rains which tried the village houses so, when the maids stood ready with mop and pail in front entries to keep the deluge out, I sat behind my door in my little house, which was all entry, and thoroughly enjoyed its protection. In one heavy thundershower the lightning struck a large pitch pine across the pond, making a very conspicuous and perfectly regular spiral groove from top to bottom, an inch or more deep, and four or five inches wide, as you would groove a walking-stick. I passed it again the other day, and was struck with awe on looking up and beholding that mark, now more distinct than ever, where a terrific and resistless bolt came down out of the harmless sky eight years ago. Men frequently say to me, "I should think you would feel lonesome down there, and want to be nearer to folks, rainy and snowy days and nights especially." I am tempted to reply to such,—This whole earth which we inhabit is but a point in space. How far apart, think you, dwell the two most distant inhabitants of yonder star, the breadth of whose disk cannot be appreciated by our instruments? Why should I feel lonely? Is not our planet in the Milky Way? This which you put seems to me not to be the most important question. What sort of space is that which separates a man from his fellows and makes him solitary? I have found that no exertion of the legs can bring two minds much nearer to one another. What do we want most to dwell near to? Not to many men surely, the depot, the post-office, the bar-room, the meeting-house, the school-house, the grocery, Beacon Hill, or the Five Points, where men most congregate, but to the perennial source of our life, whence in all our experience we have found that to issue, as the willow stands near the water and sends out its roots in that direction. This will vary with different natures, but this is the place where a wise man will dig his cellar. . . . I one evening overtook one of my townsmen, who has accumulated what is called "a handsome property,"—though I never got a *fair* view of it,—on the Walden road, driving a pair of cattle to market, who inquired of me how I could bring my mind to give up so many of the comforts of life. I answered that I was very sure I liked it passably well; I was not joking. And so I went home to my bed, and left him to pick his way through the darkness and mud to Brighton,—or Bright-town,—which place he would reach some time in the morning.

Any prospect of awakening or coming to life to a dead man makes indifferent all times and places. The place where that may occur is always the same, and indescribably pleasant to all our senses. For the most part we allow only outlying and transient circumstances to make our occasions. They are, in fact, the cause of our distraction. Nearest to all things is that power which fashions their being. *Next* to us the grandest laws are

continually being executed. *Next* to us is not the workman whom we have hired, with whom we love so well
to talk, but the workman whose work we are.

"How vast and profound is the influence of the subtile
powers of Heaven and of Earth!"

"We seek to perceive them, and we do not see them;
we seek to hear them, and we do not hear them; identi-
fied with the substance of things, they cannot be separated from them."

"They cause that in all the universe men purify and
sanctify their hearts, and clothe themselves in their holiday garments to offer sacrifices and oblations to their
ancestors. It is an ocean of subtile intelligences. They are
everywhere, above us, on our left, on our right; they
environ us on all sides."

We are the subjects of an experiment which is not a
little interesting to me. Can we not do without the society of our gossips a little while under these circumstances,—have our own thoughts to cheer us? Confucius
says truly, "Virtue does not remain as an abandoned
orphan; it must of necessity have neighbors."

With thinking we may be beside ourselves in a sane
sense. By a conscious effort of the mind we can stand
aloof from actions and their consequences; and all
things, good and bad, go by us like a torrent. We are not
wholly involved in Nature. I may be either the driftwood
in the stream, or Indra in the sky looking down on it. I
may be affected by a theatrical exhibition; on the other
hand, I *may not* be affected by an actual event which
appears to concern me much more. I only know myself
as a human entity; the scene, so to speak, of thoughts
and affections; and am sensible of a certain doubleness
by which I can stand as remote from myself as from another. However intense my experience, I am conscious
of the presence and criticism of a part of me, which, as
it were, is not a part of me, but a spectator, sharing no

experience, but taking note of it, and that is more I than it is you. When the play, it may be the tragedy, of life is over, the spectator goes his way. It was a kind of fiction, a work of the imagination only, so far as he was concerned. This doubleness may easily make us poor neighbors and friends sometimes.

I find it wholesome to be alone the greater part of the time. To be in company, even the best, is soon wearisome and dissipating. I love to be alone. I never found the companion that was so companionable as solitude.

HENRY DAVID THOREAU

WANDERLUST

To Jane: The Invitation

Best and Brightest, come away!
Fairer far than this fair day,
Which, like thee, to those in sorrow,
Comes to bid a sweet good-morrow
To the rough year just awake
In its cradle on the brake.
The brightest hour of unborn Spring
Through the winter wandering,
Found, it seems, the halcyon morn
To hoar February born;
Bending from Heaven, in azure mirth,
It kissed the forehead of the earth,
And smiled upon the silent sea,
And bade the frozen streams be free,
And waked to music all their fountains,
And breathed upon the frozen mountains,
And like a prophetess of May
Strewed flowers upon the barren way,
Making the wintry world appear
Like one on whom thou smilest, Dear.

Away, away, from men and towns,
To the wild wood and the downs—
To the silent wilderness
Where the soul need not repress
Its music, lest it should not find
An echo in another's mind,
While the touch of Nature's art
Harmonizes heart to heart.

I leave this notice on my door
For each accustomed visitor:—
"I am gone into the fields
To take what this sweet hour yields;—
Reflection, you may come to-morrow,
Sit by the fireside with Sorrow.—
You with the unpaid bill, Despair,—
You tiresome verse-reciter, Care,—
I will pay you in the grave,—
Death will listen to your stave.
Expectation too, be off!
To-day is for itself enough;
Hope, in pity mock not Woe
With smiles, nor follow where I go;
Long having lived on thy sweet food,
At length I find one moment's good
After long pain—with all your love,
This you never told me of."

Radiant Sister of the Day
Awake! arise! and come away!
To the wild woods and the plains,
To the pools where winter rains
Image all their roof of leaves,
Where the pine its garland weaves
Of sapless green, and ivy dun,
Round stems that never kiss the sun;

Where the lawns and pastures be,
And the sandhills of the sea;—
Where the melting hoar-frost wets
The daisy-star that never sets,
And wind-flowers, and violets,
Which yet join not scent to hue,
Crown the pale year weak and new;
When the night is left behind
In the deep east, dun and blind,
And the blue noon is over us,
And the multitudinous
Billows murmur at our feet,
Where the earth and ocean meet,
And all things seem only one
In the universal sun.

PERCY BYSSHE SHELLEY

THE LAKE ISLE OF INNISFREE

I will arise and go now, and go to Innisfree,
And a small cabin build there, of clay and wattles made:
Nine bean-rows will I have there, a hive for the honey-
bee,
And live alone in the bee-loud glade.

And I shall have some peace there, for peace comes
dropping slow,
Dropping from the veils of the morning to where the
cricket sings;
There midnight's all a glimmer, and noon a purple glow,
And evening full of the linnet's wings.

I will arise and go now, for always night and day
I hear lake water lapping with low sounds by the shore;
While I stand on the roadway, or on the pavements grey,
I hear it in the deep heart's core.

W. B. YEATS

From ON GOING A JOURNEY

One of the pleasantest things in the world is going a journey; but I like to go by myself. I can enjoy society in a room; but out of doors, nature is company enough for me. I am then never less alone than when alone.

"The fields his study, nature was his book."

I cannot see the wit of walking and talking at the same time. When I am in the country I wish to vegetate like the country. I am not for criticizing hedge-rows and black cattle. I go out of town in order to forget the town and all that is in it. There are those who for this purpose go to watering-places, and carry the metropolis with them. I like more elbow-room and fewer incumbrances. I like solitude, when I give myself up to it, for the sake of solitude; nor do I ask for

"a friend in my retreat,
Whom I may whisper solitude is sweet."

The soul of a journey is liberty, perfect liberty, to think, feel, do, just as one pleases. We go a journey chiefly to be free of all impediments and of all inconveniences; to leave ourselves behind, much more to get rid of others. It is because I want a little breathing-space to muse on indifferent matters, where Contemplation

"May plume her feathers and let grow her wings,
That in the various bustle of resort
Were all too ruffled, and sometimes impair'd,"

that I absent myself from the town for a while, without feeling at a loss the moment I am left by myself. Instead of a friend in a post-chaise or in a Tilbury, to exchange good things with, and vary the same stale topics over again, for once let me have a truce with impertinence.

Give me the clear blue sky over my head, and the green turf beneath my feet, a winding road before me, and three hours' march to dinner—and then to thinking! It is hard if I cannot start some game on these lone heaths. I laugh, I run, I leap, I sing for joy. From the point of yonder rolling cloud I plunge into my past being, and revel there, as the sun-burnt Indian plunges headlong into the wave that wafts him to his native shore. Then long-forgotten things, like "sunken wrack and sumless treasuries," burst upon my eager sight, and I begin to feel, think, and be myself again. Instead of an awkward silence, broken by attempts at wit or dull common-places mine is that undisturbed silence of the heart which alone is perfect eloquence. . . .

WILLIAM HAZLITT

Age

I was standing on the veranda of Meg's graciously attractive house in Cuernavaca not too long ago, waiting with some friends to get started on a sunset picnic we had planned at the pyramids of the sun and moon, a half hour's ride away, when Eduardo, a neighbor of Meg's, came across the garden. His gait was somewhat slow, and his shoulders stooped just a tiny bit. His silver-white hair contrasted attractively with his bronzed Mayan face. His bright blue eyes glistened as he approached, and his mouth was spread in a warm smile of greeting that made minute genial creases around the outer corners of his eyes.

Once, before the Mexican Revolution, Eduardo's family had been wealthy hacendados of Yucatán. Eduardo had spent a good part of his early life living and traveling abroad. His English is perfect. He spends most of his time now enjoying the semi-tropical greenery of Cuernavaca and the mountains that surround it, reading and re-reading the books he has collected from all parts of the world. We exchanged the usual pleasantries and then he told me he wasn't going on the picnic because he thought the evening air might be a little too chilly for him. We were having an unusually cold spell at the time. "The worst in fifty years," Eduardo said. Then, not at all defensively, he remarked that he was nearing eighty, and one of the pleasures of old age was that he didn't have to go anywhere he didn't want to. "The last fifteen years have been the happiest and most serene of my life," he said. "Old age is wonderful. I know that may be hard to believe. But I do as I please, read when I please. Of course, I have my frailties. I couldn't run down the street. But the compensations more than make up for that. You're too young to understand," he concluded with a mischievous smile.

Well, at sixty-five I don't consider myself a chicken exactly. But Eduardo wouldn't listen to my protestations. That seems to be another of the pleasures of age. You can be absolutely sure that you are right. And you don't care whether or not anyone else agrees with you. I haven't reached that happy state yet. But I must say that I have begun to understand what Eduardo was talking about. Certainly, Eduardo has overcome one of the great fears of life, probably the second greatest fear we have, the fear of growing old. The greatest fear is death. I don't know why we should fear our own mortality so much; I think it is too bad that death isn't accepted as part of life.

And it's really about time that age was accepted as part of life too. One of the paradoxes of our contemporary civilization is that so much of medical science and research is directed toward the prolonging of life that the average life expectancy keeps going up steadily, yet we are afraid of growing old. And many of us spend more than half our waking hours trying to camouflage our age.

It is a pleasure to look at the serene beauty of the faces of the aging Indian women in Mexico. They are free of the lines of tension I am used to seeing on the faces of women back home. Whether they are coming out of the Colony after lunch or are on their way to Elizabeth Arden or wherever they go for their facials and massages, they all have that haunted and drawn and strained look. They have gone to a fine restaurant and they have eaten Melba toast, chicken broth, and grapefruit. I am not criticizing their concern about their outside appearance, but it seems to me that that concern is deeper than just being worried about middleaged spread and bulges. It is the awful fear of growing old. This fear is not limited just to women. In fact, I sometimes think that men have it a great deal more than women. I know that my husband had it. And Ben Hecht, with whom Charlie collaborated on plays, had it. Ben was always working on himself to hold back age or the appearance of age. I know that women need to be fashionable and want to keep their figures trim. But I also know there is nothing more beautiful than an unadorned old face with the lines that tell a story, a story of a life that has been lived with some fullness. I don't care whether it's a life that has been lived in goodness or in mischief, if it has been lived fully there is an interesting and arresting quality in that face—in those lines that life has written there.

This effort to turn back or hold back the clock is one of the most pathetic efforts in which people engage. So many people fail to learn that there is no road back, that you cannot repeat things. Many years ago, George C. Tyler, the producer who helped make me a star and who guided much of my education during the years of our association, introduced me to the works of Leonard Merrick, who was more highly regarded then than he is today. One of his books was called

Conrad in Quest of His Youth, an account of how the aging hero had tried to retrace and recapture a part of his youth. One segment describes Conrad's attempts to rekindle an old romance that had taken place in the beautiful French city of Rouen. At the end the woman, realizing the futility of the effort, departs while Conrad is sleeping. She leaves a note that reads, "Farewell, dear dreamer, there is no road back to Rouen." The phrase, "there's no road back to Rouen" was one of the maxims of our household and wherever it has been possible I have tried to abide by its wisdom. I have never tried to repeat things I've done, not even in the theater. I've never, never wanted to revive any of the plays in which I have appeared. I've never wanted to go back and do a play, for example, like *Victoria Regina*, though I've been asked many times. I was asked to do it on the screen and I would not do that either. I have learned that it is best to leave a memory alone.

When I was young, of course, the idea of growing old never crossed my mind. It just didn't seem possible to me. Ah, youth. Well, when I look around me, I wonder how many old people have learned what Eduardo has learned, that old age can be wonderful, assuming that one's health is good and there is the absence of want.

CICERO'S ADVICE FOR THE AGING

To those who have no resources in themselves for living well and happily, every age is burdensome, but to those who seek all good things from themselves nothing can appear evil which the necessity of nature entails, in which class particularly is old age, which all men wish to attain, and yet they complain of it when they have attained it; so great is the inconsistency of waywardness and folly.

The fittest arms of old age are the attainment and practice of the virtues; which, if cultivated at every period of life, produce wonderful fruits when you have lived to a great age . . .

They advance no arguments who say that old age is not engaged in active duty and resemble those who say that the pilot in navigation is unemployed, for that while some climb the mast, others run up and down the deck, others empty the bilgewater, he, holding the helm, sits at the stern at his ease.

He does not do the things that the young men do, but in truth, he does much greater and better things.

Great actions are not achieved by great exertion of strength or speed or quick movements of the body but by talent, authority and judgment, which faculties old age, is usually so far from being deprived, that it is even improved in them.

But in my whole discourse remember that I am praising that old age which is established on the foundations of youth . . . neither grey hairs nor wrinkles can suddenly catch respect but the former part of life honorably spent reaps the fruit of authority at the close.

Whatever time is assigned to each to live, with that he ought to be content . . . for a short period of life is long enough for living well and honorably, and if you should advance further, you need no more grieve than farmers do when the loveliness of spring time has passed, that summer and autumn have come.

If any God should grant me that from this period of life I should become a child again and cry in the cradle I should earnestly refuse it, nor in truth should I like, having run, as it were, my course, to be called back to the starting place from the goal.

Neither do I regret that I have lived since I have lived in such a way that I conceive I was not born in vain, and from this life I depart as from a temporary lodging, not as from a home, for nature has assigned us to it as an inn to sojourn in, not a place of habitation . . .

THE FABLE OF WOMAN'S TRUE FRIEND AND THE HOPEFUL ANTIQUE

The Beauty Doctor sat in her Pink Reception Room hoping that she resembled her Lithographs. Her Income was a Dollar every time she took a Full Breath. She got it by selling Freckle Food and a Preparation for getting rid of Moles, called Moline. Her hot Specialty was to Calcimine the Has-Beens and feed them a little Ginger and send them into the Arena looking like Vassar Girls. It did not take her long to put an Extension on an Eye-Brow, and she could provide a Blush for those who had been going to Card Parties so long that they had forgotten how to Blush. When she got after a Wild Hair the Hair simply threw up both Hands and quit. In a little Folder entitled "How to Fool Everybody except those who live in the Same House," she had proved that there was no Reason why a Girl of 60 should not look 19 if she put on enough Shellac and kept out of the Light.

The Beauty Doctor had seen many a Derelict float in for a new Coat of Armor Plate, but the Nobody's Darling that wafted in this Day established a Record. She was something like Poultry. That is, if she carried any Adipose, it did not show in her Face or Feet. And she wouldn't have torn under the Wing. She had a Bird's-Eye Maple Complexion and wore one of these Gowns that you get by measuring yourself with a String and sending Two Dollars. Without saying anything in Disparagement of her Private Character or denying that she may have been kind to her Relations, it may be added that she resembled a Daily Hint from the Short Timber.

"I saw your Card in the Bee-Keepers' Bazaar, and I have decided to back in for a few Repairs," said the Visitor. "If you can build me a Set of Curves the same as I see in the Cigarette Pictures and cause my Hair to Bush out and hang to the Belt Line the same as it used to in 1882, and give me some perfumed Dope that will restore a Peaches and Cream Complexion on or before May 1st, I will do the Generous Thing by you and pay Seven Dollars."

The Beauty Doctor seldom took the Count, but this was one of the Times. "My Private Secretary will take charge of your Case," she said faintly, and then she went into another Apartment and lay down.

The Private Secretary was the Last Resort. He had no Conscience. For two seasons he had been a Cloak Salesman. "Surely you have not come here for Treatment," he said, smiling at the Caller. "You have the Shape that they are raving about in Paree this Spring, and we could not improve your general Tint no matter how many Coats we used. The quiet and unobtrusive Elegance of your Get-Up, combined with what Nature has so generously parcelled out to you, makes it unnecessary to attempt any Alterations. All that you need to do is to retain intact your present Category of Superlative Charms. This you can manage by a careful Perusal of our Book: 'How to stay Pretty.' It comes to Ten Louies."

So she had the Volume wrapped up and went away tickled.

Moral: *The only Ones who need Patching are those who Think they need it.*

GEORGE ADE

WHAT ARE YEARS?

What is our innocence,
what is our guilt? All are
    naked, none is safe. And whence
is courage: the unanswered question,
the resolute doubt—
dumbly calling, deafly listening—that
in misfortune, even death,
        encourages others
        and in its defeat, stirs

    the soul to be strong? He
sees deep and is glad, who
    accedes to mortality
and in his imprisonment, rises
upon himself as
the sea in a chasm, struggling to be
free and unable to be,
        in its surrendering
        finds its continuing.

    So he who strongly feels,
behaves. The very bird,
    grown taller as he sings, steels
his form straight up. Though he is captive,
his mighty singing
says, satisfaction is a lowly
thing, how pure a thing is joy.
        This is mortality,
        this is eternity.

                                MARIANNE MOORE

ARTIFICIAL BEAUTY

You give your cheeks a rosy stain,
  With washes dye your hair,
But paint and washes both are vain
  To give a youthful air.

Those wrinkles mock your daily toil;
  No labor will efface them;
You wear a mask of smoothest oil,
  Yet still with ease we trace them.

An art so fruitless then forsake,
  Which though you much excel in,
You never can contrive to make
  Old Hecuba young Helen.

LUCIANUS

WHEN YOU ARE OLD

When you are old and grey and full of sleep,
And nodding by the fire, take down this book,
And slowly read, and dream of the soft look
Your eyes had once, and of their shadows deep;

How many loved your moments of glad grace,
And loved your beauty with love false or true,
But one man loved the pilgrim soul in you,
And loved the sorrows of your changing face;

And bending down beside the glowing bars,
Murmur, a little sadly, how Love fled
And paced upon the mountains overhead
And hid his face amid a crowd of stars.

W. B. YEATS

From THE SUMMING UP

I look forward to old age without dismay. When Lawrence of Arabia was killed I read in an article contributed by a friend that it was his habit to ride his motorbicycle at an excessive speed with the notion that an accident would end his life while he was still in full possession of his powers and so spare him the indignity of old age. If this is true it was a great weakness in that strange and somewhat theatrical character. It showed want of sense. For the complete life, the perfect pattern, includes old age as well as youth and maturity. The beauty of the morning and the radiance of noon are good, but it would be a very silly person who drew the curtains and turned on the light in order to shut out the tranquillity of the evening. Old age has its pleasures, which, though different, are not less than the pleasures of youth. The philosophers have always told us that we are the slaves of our passions, and is it so small a thing to be liberated from their sway? The fool's old age will be foolish, but so was his youth. The young man turns away from it with horror because he thinks that when he reaches it, he will still yearn for the things that give variety and gusto to his youth. He is mistaken. It is true that the old man will no longer be able to climb an Alp or tumble a pretty girl on a bed; it is true that he can no longer arouse the concupiscence of others. It is something to be free from the pangs of unrequited love and the torment of jealousy. It is something that envy, which so often poisons youth, should be assuaged by the extinction of desire. But these are negative compensations; old age has positive compensations also. Paradoxical as it may sound it has more time. When I was young I was amazed at Plutarch's statement that the elder Cato began at the age of eighty to learn Greek. I am amazed no longer. Old age is ready to undertake tasks that youth shirked because they would take too long. In old age the taste improves and it is possible to enjoy art and literature without the personal bias that in youth warps the judgment. It has the satisfaction of its own fulfilment. It is liberated from the trammels of human egoism; free at last, the soul delights in the passing moment, but does not bid it stay. It has completed the pattern. Goethe asked for survival after death so that he might realize those sides of himself which he felt that in his life he had not time to develop. But did he not say that he who would accomplish anything must learn to limit himself? When you read his life you cannot but be struck by the way in which he wasted time in trivial pursuits. Perhaps if he had limited himself more carefully he would have developed everything that properly belonged to his special individuality and so found no need of a future life.

W. SOMERSET MAUGHAM

Work

CHILDBIRTH is easy compared to giving birth to a role in a play. The work is intense and exhausting, whether you are playing an active part that requires great physical effort or a sedentary role such as the one created by Katharine Cornell in *The Barretts of Wimpole Street*, in which she sat on a sofa the whole time she was on the stage. You go home from rehearsals with your feet aching, and your back aching and your head aching—and usually your soul—because every muscle and every nerve in you has been strained toward that goal of capturing the essence of the character you are trying to interpret. And sometimes that essence eludes you for too long, and sometimes, oh God, you never catch it.

Indeed, I sometimes think there may be nothing harder. It is harder than the task of the creative writer, who can put off his work when he doesn't feel up to it. The actor in rehearsal can't do that. He must plow on, force, push, go on in spite of his rebellious mind and spirit.

Probably the most onerous of all things connected with rehearsal is the need, when you have gone home tired, to keep working instead of relaxing and turning to other things, to keep studying your lines, learning all the new ones that the playwright had to write the day before. The time comes when you hate every word of the play and you wonder how you ever got into it. I have never accepted the idea that there is such a thing as "a poor study" in the theater—that actor who can't memorize lines. I think that the only time you can't memorize is when you refuse to face up to the deadly grind of study.

And the work isn't over even after the play has opened. Actors are incurable seekers. They are always searching after some perfection in their roles that rarely can be attained. I remember an interview that Lynn Fontanne once gave in which she described how she and her husband, Alfred Lunt, go home after a performance and continue to work, becoming more and more acquainted with the roles they are playing, studying every inflection, every intonation. "This," she said, "is a process that goes on all through the run of the play."

Even now, as I was making the selections of my favorite scenes for this book, I was overcome with pangs of misgivings, even horror, as I read over those plays. Repeatedly, I found myself plagued and unsettled by such thoughts as, "Oh, how I said that line; Oh, I overdid that one badly; Oh, if only I could have a chance at that part again."

More often than not, however, we actors must console ourselves with the thought that somehow, somewhere we have gotten close enough to our vision to satisfy the audience even if we have not completely satisfied ourselves. Still, with each new role there springs the hope that *it* may be the one with which the challenge will be fully met. That hope of conquest—and not the money or anything else—is what lures us on until we're exhausted and lying flat on our faces with weariness from the struggle through the years.

It is good to be able to quit when the spirit is weary or one's work no longer brings the desired results. For actors, sadly, quitting is exceptionally hard. For one thing, they are notoriously profligate and generous with their money, and too often the tired years are accompanied by empty pockets. And for another thing, they wouldn't be actors if the instinct for giving, for spending, weren't strong within them. Acting *is* giving. We say an actor *gives* a performance, and I would add that wrapped up in that performance is a part of himself which he presents with love to those who have come to receive it. Maybe that sounds lofty—particularly if applied to actors in nondescript roles, some of whom have spent their lives in them. But after years of watching, I know for a truth that an actor, be he star or bit player, famous or obscure, approaches each performance with the wild hope in his heart that he will find something better of himself to give to his role and his audience that night than he found the night before. It has always seemed a kind of miracle to me—this giving of self, which is acting.

In my youth, I used to wonder how people could bear not being actors, and as the long years of work stretched out, I began to wonder how I would bear not being an actress when the time came for me to exit gracefully from the theater. One doesn't want to hang about too long, pressing upon the world the gifts that have become a little damaged or tarnished by envious time.

Through the years, as opening nights have become harder, I have tried to prolong my stretches of idleness, but I find I approach idleness as strenuously as I had always approached work. I literally attack it, until exhausted friends start urging me back into plays so we can all relax. I know now that I shall always be at work at something, for I have come to realize that work is an essential of life.

I have read that working-age people are going to have an unprecedented amount of time on their hands because of automation. Ernest Havemann notes that "Dr. Richard Bellman, a mathematician at the Rand Corporation predicts that no later than twenty-five years from now two per cent of our population will be able to produce all our goods and food that the other 98 per cent can possibly consume. And economist Marion Clawson estimates that Americans will have *660 billion* more hours of leisure in the year 2000 than they did in 1950. What will we do with all this spare time? Will it be a blessing or a bane?"

It hardly will be a blessing to those unable to cope with it. Nothing is more pathetic than men who have dreamed of retirement and then find that the idleness for which they have yearned has become a bitter thing in the declining years of their lives. You can see these men in places like Bayfront Park in downtown Miami. Edwin A. Lahey, a newspaperman, observed in one of his stories, "there should be an air of euphoria ascending from the luxuriant verdure of this park. But you feel, instead of a sense of well being, loneliness and desolation. Retired people come here. They bring their restlessness, their sense of uselessness. They sit immobilized on the benches before the band stand, on the benches scattered throughout the park. Some of them gab about the past with others. Some of them just sit, gazing into the distance."

We are told that individuals already enjoying leisure are filling this time by following a variety of pursuits such as boating, skin-diving, and skiing, and by increasing attendance at spectator sports. A recent Gallup report indicated that ten million Americans have found time to be amateur painters, eleven million to be amateur musicians. For hours visitors stood in line to look at the *Mona Lisa* when it was exhibited in New York, and book publishing has become a billion-dollar-a-year business. This is fine as long as people make a really serious effort to work at these things, to probe and study. The important thing is that we must not be fooled, nor fool ourselves. Even at our pleasures, it is necessary to work.

Here are a short essay by Ida M. Tarbell and an excerpt from a letter written by H. L. Mencken to Will Durant that express exactly what I feel.

WORK

The most satisfying interest in my life, books and friends and beauty aside, is work—plain hard steady work. It is for work—books and friends and beauty again aside—that I shall be most grateful on Thanksgiving Day of 1936. As I have been at it for fifty-six of my seventy-nine years, I feel that I have given it a fair trial.

What do I get out of it?

I have no illusions about its nature. If work is to be productive—that is, give the worker something he can exchange for the products of other workers—it is no sinecure. It carries with it fatigue, disappointment, failure, revolt.

I have never in my life undertaken a fresh piece of work that I have not been obliged to take myself by the scruff of the neck and seat myself at my desk and keep my hand on the scruff until my revolt had subsided. That is, I know the difficulties in steady work. If there was nothing in it but the fruits of barter, I would rather trust myself to the road. On the road you can at least go South in winter and North in summer.

But the ability to barter is the least of work's satisfactions, necessary as that may be, great as may be the sense of dignity which a worker gets from being economically independent, joyous as may be the fun of having money to spend, to give, perhaps to waste.

Highest, perhaps, in the satisfactions work gives is the sense that you are keeping in step with the nature of things. That may sound esoteric, but it is plain fact. This is a working universe. So far as we know, it has been that since the beginning of things. There is no spot in it which stands still. Every star is on the move. Such a reliable universe, too: every planet in its place, doing its task; every eclipse on the minute.

Here on earth everything works—the grain of sand, the oaks, the clouds—works and incessantly changes, passing from one form to another, for nothing dies as a fact. The earth tolerates no dead beats; it keeps everything busy. If it did not it would be out of step in the universe in which it travels year in and out, never behindhand, never off the track—sunrise and sunset, moonrise and moonset always on schedule.

If I am to be happy in this steady-working world I must work, too; otherwise I'll suffer discomfort, uneasiness akin to that which comes to me when in walking I cannot keep step with my companion, when in talking I cannot follow the argument or catch the meaning, when in singing I am off key.

There is a vast unhappiness, inexplicable to those it afflicts, which comes from idleness in a working world. The idle are self-destructive as would be a star which announced that it was going to stand still for an eon or two.

What the idler fails to understand is the beauty of rhythm, the beauty and the excitement of being in his place in the endless chain of creative motion which is the essential nature of this magnificent and incomprehensible universe.

There is no mystification about this. It is as plain a fact as anything we know, and we ignore it to the destruction of our peace of mind, if not to the peril of our lives. It is one of the factors in our situation on earth which must be accepted.

Margaret Fuller Ossoli once announced loftily that she accepted the universe. "She better," commented Ralph Waldo Emerson. We better, or the first thing we know the world will spew us out of its mouth as the universe does a revolting star, breaking it to fragments doomed eternally to cruise through space. Fragments occasionally collide with a planet, burying themselves in its surface—meteorites, we call them. They are pieces (probably!) of a star that tried to get out of work assigned it.

Work means health. The very urges of our bodies show that nature expects action of us if we are to be in health. From the time we kick our heels and try our lungs on being released from our mother's womb we cry for work. Watch the child—never still. It is obeying the order of nature to keep busy.

How defeated and restless the child that is not doing something in which it sees a purpose, a meaning! It is by its self-directed activity that the child, as years pass, finds its work, the thing it wants to do and for which it finally is willing to deny itself pleasure, ease, even sleep and comfort.

In such work comes perhaps the deepest of all work's satisfactions: the consciousness that you are growing, the realization that gradually there is more skill in your fingers and your mind. If you work steadily, persistently, with a conviction of the necessity of effort if you are to be in harmony with the nature of things, you grow.

You do more. By giving yourself freely to your work

you become a creator suggesting new techniques, new machines, finding new magic in words, new arrangements of facts and thoughts.

Here lies the worker's salvation when the road he has been following suddenly ends—when the factory, the shop, the office closes. The worker who realizes that he has something to do with the making of new work when the old ends does not sit down by the roadside and cry for someone to take down the barriers. He strikes across the open fields, chops a path through the woods, seizes any odd job he spies, labors to set his own notions in operation.

Thousands of men and women have done that in these last difficult seven years and are coming to Thanksgiving Day blessing the Lord for their larger sense of the nature of work, their obligation to create it, keep it going. Thrown out, they refused to beg it—they set about to make it.

They have learned a fundamental truth—that the creative force in work must be constantly exercised, never checked or tampered with, if work is to be kept abundant, if its wornout forms are to be constantly replaced with those which are higher, finer, more productive.

With growth and creation come satisfactions of new kinds. Your work fits in with the work of others. You know yourself to be finally a part of that working world which produces sound things for sound purposes.

But work does more for you. It is the chief protection you have in suffering, despair, disillusionment, fear. There is no antidote to mental and spiritual uncertainty and pain like a regular job.

Here, then, is my philosophy of work—the reasons why after fifty-six years of unbroken trial I thank God for it. It is something which reaches the deepest needs, helps reconcile the baffling mystery of the universe, helps establish order in a disorderly society; which puts despair to sleep, gives experience to offer that youth who is willing to believe you too once were young and had his problems, gives a platter of fruit—small though it may be—to divide with those who for one or another reason have no fruit on their platter.

Blessed work! There will be no finer fruit on our Thanksgiving table.

IDA M. TARBELL

From A LETTER WRITTEN BY H. L. MENCKEN TO WILL DURANT

You ask me, in brief, what satisfaction I get out of life, and why I go on working. I go on working for the same reason that a hen goes on laying eggs. There is in every living creature an obscure but powerful impulse to active functioning. Life demands to be lived. Inaction, save as a measure of recuperation between bursts of activity, is painful and dangerous to the healthy organism—in fact, it is almost impossible. Only the dying can be really idle.

The precise form of an individual's activity is determined, of course, by the equipment with which he came into the world. In other words, it is determined by his heredity. I do not lay eggs, as a hen does, because I was born without any equipment for it. For the same reason I do not get myself elected to Congress, or play the violoncello, or teach metaphysics in a college, or work in a steel mill. What I do is simply what lies easiest to my hand. It happens that I was born with an intense and insatiable interest in ideas, and thus like to play with them. It happens also that I was born with rather more than the average facility for putting them into words. In consequence, I am a writer and editor, which is to say, a dealer in them and concoctor of them.

There is very little conscious volition in all this. What

I do was ordained by the inscrutable fates, not chosen by me. In my boyhood, yielding to a powerful but still subordinate interest in exact facts, I wanted to be a chemist, and at the same time my poor father tried to make me a business man. At other times, like any other relatively poor man, I have longed to make a lot of money by some easy swindle. But I became a writer all the same, and shall remain one until the end of the chapter, just as a cow goes on giving milk all her life, even though what appears to be her self-interest urges her to give gin. . . .

A Gift of Joy

WHEN I read poetry I expect sensual pleasure from the sounds of the words. But I also want to be arrested by what is being said: the philosophy of the poetry, the thinking of the poet. This, of course, means that the poets I like are those I can understand, those who make patterns that are familiar to me. And so my poets are the ones who speak to me with clarity and innocence and beauty.

My insistence upon uplift and affirmation almost sounds as if I have an inner core of despair and that I am trying awfully hard to rise above it. I don't think this is so. I think I was born with a happy spirit. I remember one day, when I was about twelve or thirteen, having been sent for by my beloved English teacher, Sister Mary Eileen. As I walked into her room, she suddenly burst out laughing. She said, "Whenever you are about to come in here I am prepared to call you the most dreadful names, but, instead, I find myself wanting to call you Mary Sunshine because you always enter with your smiling and dancing eyes, and walking on your toes. What is it, why do you do this?" And I didn't know. I guess that is just the way I have always walked at life. I've always approached life with affection and with admiration. I'm a great admirer of the world and what goes on in it, even though, God knows, I don't blind myself to the dark and bleak and despairing. But I refuse to berate myself and scold myself or constantly whine at the way of the world. And I don't want my poets to whine either, which too many have been doing for too long—those moaners over the human condition, the complainers about man's plight. This is only the partial vision. My poets have the gift of joy, they are the ones who can see things whole, who can sense and comprehend the vast scheme that has been designed for us.

As Lillian Smith has pointed out, "Only the poet can look beyond details at the total picture; only the poet can feel the courage beyond fear, only he can grasp the splinters and make a new wholeness that does not yet exist. It is his job to think in spans of ten thousand years; his job to feel the slow movement of the human spirit evolving; to see that the moment is close for all mankind to make another leap forward; it is his job to scoop up the debris of our times and show us the giant outlines of the human spirit becoming more able to relate to the unknown and the unseen."

It seems to me that too many of our writers are bent on displaying a world in which, as one critic observed, "man is degraded, crushed, mashed, thrown to his knees, trampled underfoot into the ground," a world doomed to inevitable catastrophe. These writers, putting on their gloomy shrouds are, as Lillian Smith described them, "giving us fragmented sketches of sick people," holding "before us in play and story a never-ending view of miserable, lost, lonely schizophrenics." She went on to say, "Of course we should look with

compassion and understanding at our sick and lost ones—
young and old—but they should not be presented to us in
drama and novel as though they are the *whole of contemporary life*, as though they are *all we have to count on* for the
future.

"Here is where poets turn to demagogues: by the use of
the big lie they, too, become exploiters; they, too, are guilty
of arousing fear and despair. Just as does the demagogue,
they too, treat *hope* as the four-letter word you must never
be caught using. They, like the demagogues, destroy by tear-
ing up purpose, by calling the human condition an absurdity,
judging it by weeks and decades, failing to see far enough
into the future to find anytring worthy of effort on the part
of the intelligent ones. And what effect does this have on the
young? All we need do is look around us: at the beats and
the smokers of pot and the kids in high school who are now
drug addicts and the young homosexuals flaunting their de-
viations. They are the characters in the plays now come to
life; they are now acting out in real homes and real streets
the splintered fantasies the novelists wrote about. Our writers, our poets and dramatists have forgotten what every real
artist knows: men imitate art, art does not imitate men."

I look to the poets, as Hesiod did, to give to man a scene
worth imitating, an ideal worth striving for.

Since it is because of the Muses and far darting Apollo
that there should be poets and harp players upon this
earth. Kings are made by Zeus, but happy is the man
whom the Muses love. Sweet are the words that flow
from his mouth. For although a man, in his newly dis-
tressed soul, may suffer sorrow and have fear because
his heart is troubled, yet when a poet, the servant of
the Muses, hymns the famous deeds of men of old or
the blessed gods who live in Olympus, then suddenly

he forgets his heavy-heartedness and remembers no
more the worries that oppressed him. Yet the gifts of
the Muses pass all too rapidly away.

I often wonder: Who will pick up the pieces of our damaged world? A poet, I think . . .

When Nature the unending thread devises,
Upon indifferent whirling spools to spin,
When from all creatures' clashing mass arises
A sullen and discordant din—
Who cleaves the dull monotonous gyration
And into living rhythms divides the whole,
Who calls the singular to general consecration
Wherein the chords accordant nobly roll,
Who shapes the storm as symbol of our passion,
In thoughtful souls lets sunset glow be red,
Who rifles all the floral spring to fashion
A path for the beloved's tread,
Who plucks the green leaves without form or meaning
To be as crowns of human honor sealed,
Unites the gods from safe Olympus leaning?
Man's power in the poet's soul revealed.

JOHANN WOLFGANG VON GOETHE